Grade
4

Summer Activities
for the Gifted Student

Written by **Kathleen Hex**

Illustrations by **John Haslam**

FlashK*i*ds

An imprint of Sterling Children's Books

FLASH KIDS, STERLING, and the distinctive Sterling logo are registered trademarks of Sterling Publishing Co., Inc.

Published by Sterling Publishing Co., Inc.
387 Park Avenue South, New York, NY 10016
Text and illustrations © 2010 by Flash Kids
Distributed in Canada by Sterling Publishing
c/o Canadian Manda Group, 165 Dufferin Street
Toronto, Ontario, Canada M6K 3H6
Distributed in the United Kingdom by GMC Distribution Services
Castle Place, 166 High Street, Lewes, East Sussex, England BN7 1XU
Distributed in Australia by Capricorn Link (Australia) Pty. Ltd.
P.O. Box 704, Windsor, NSW 2756, Australia

Cover image © Wayne Eardley/Radius Images/Corbis
Cover design and production by Mada Design, Inc.

Sterling ISBN 978-1-4114-2764-8

Manufactured in Canada

Lot #:
2 4 6 8 10 9 7 5 3
02/12

For information about custom editions, special sales, premium and
corporate purchases, please contact Sterling Special Sales
Department at 800-805-5489 or specialsales@sterlingpublishing.com.

Learning doesn't have to stop when the school year ends. *Summer Activities for the Gifted Student* offers thought-provoking exercises designed to challenge advanced learners during the vacation months. It reviews familiar skills and introduces new ones, all the while providing your child with the intellectual stimulation gifted children crave.

This workbook provides activities that challenge your child's unique abilities in all subject areas—language arts, math, social studies, and science. All materials presented here are carefully calibrated to match the average reading level, analytical capability, and subject interest of a gifted fourth grader. Reading passages present new vocabulary, math problems encourage critical-thinking skills, and writing exercises promote creativity. Science and social studies activities introduce new concepts while testing logic and problem-solving skills.

A few activities in this book will require finding additional information using outside sources such as an encyclopedia, a dictionary, or the Internet. Helping your child complete these exercises provides an opportunity to teach valuable research skills. In fact, all of the activities in this book provide a chance to work with your child to offer advice, guidance, praise, and encouragement. Have a wonderful summer and, most of all, have fun learning with your child!

The Right Light

Replace each word entry with a word from the *-ight* word family.

1. **argument:** a disagreement between two people

2. **enjoyment:** a source of pleasure

3. **departure:** travel

4. **small:** slender, slim, narrow

5. **afraid:** fearful

6. **power:** ability to do something or affect something

7. **view:** range of vision

8. **radiant:** shining, shimmering

9. **taut:** tense, not slack

10. **illuminate:** to brighten

fight
delight
flight
slight
fright
might
sight
bright
tight
light

Dictionary

Lucky Ticket

Read the number and write it in another way.

1. | 96 | ninety-six

2. | 75 |

3. | 6,375 |

4. | 1,286 |

5. | 6,604 |

6. | 4,070 |

Name the next number and write it two ways.

7. 35: _____36_____   _____thirty-six_____

8. 9,988: _____9,989_____   _____

9. 5,040: _____5,041_____

Name the previous number and write it two ways.

10. 97: _____96_____   _____ninety-six_____

11. 3,200: _____3,199_____   _____

12. 6,375: _____6,374_____

Energy from the Sun

Energy from the sun can be used to make heat and electric power. This is called solar energy. This energy can be changed into electric power in two different ways.

One way to use solar energy is with a solar cell. Solar cells change light energy into electric energy. When sunlight hits a solar cell, it makes electric charges flow through layers of a special material that produces a useful current. Have you ever used a solar calculator? It was powered with a solar cell. These cells are used in small things like watches and calculators, and big ones like spacecraft and satellites. Solar cells can also bring electric power to places where there are no power lines.

Another way to generate electric power from the sun is by collecting and using its heat. Large mirrors are used to catch the sunlight and direct it at a pipe or metal container filled with a liquid. The heat from the sun causes the liquid to reach temperatures up to 30 times hotter than boiling water. This heat makes steam. The steam runs an engine called a steam turbine. The steam turbine creates electric power.

Answer the questions about the reading.

1. What are the two major ways solar rays can be changed into electric energy?

Soler energy, using its heat watches and calcclators.

2. What kinds of things are powered by solar cells? _____

_____

3. Where might it be useful to have a house powered by solar energy? _____

_____

4. Do you think using solar energy is a good idea? Why or why not? _____

_____

_____

_____

Spelling in Space

Circle the correct spelling of the word that matches the definition.

1. more than one   pulral   plural   prual

2. movable items in an office or home   furniture   fruniture   furnitrue

3. something that is good or
advantageous   benefit   benifit   benafit

4. to compute   calculat   caculate   calculate

5. to argue or debate   despute   daspute   dispute

6. knowledge gained from enduring
something   expereince   experience   expirience

7. the smallest physical unit of
an element   molecule   molacule   mollecule

8. a letter other than a vowel   consanant   consonnant   consonant

9. essential or required   necessary   neccessary   neccesary

10. a unit of measure to describe
warmth or coldness   temparature   temprature   temperature

11. what an object consists of   substince   substence   substance

12. a specific person or thing   partacular   particular   partcluar

Up, Up, and Away

Compare each pair using <, >, or = signs.

1. 75  99

2. 1,326  1,300

3. 9,099  9,909

4. 2,220  2,220

5. 6,750  7,650

6. 8,009  8,080

7. 4,112  4,012

8. 3,310 3,310

9. five thousand, forty-nine five thousand, four hundred ninety

10. seven thousand, seven hundred sixty-six  seven thousand, sixty-six

Fill in the blank with the closest possible whole number.

11. 65< ___ 66___

12. 4,749= _____

13. 752= _____

14. _____ <8,622

15. _____ >3,100

16. 7,000< _____

17. _____ <1,199

18. _____ >999

19. 10,000> _____

20. _____ <50

A River of Riddles

Use a word from the word bank to answer each riddle.

forest	valley	gulf
ocean	peninsula	desert
island	lake	hill

1. This is a barren area with very little rainfall. Plants that live in this area do not require much water. _____

2. This body of water is salty and partially surrounded by land. _____

3. This area of land is covered with lots of trees and underbrush. It requires adequate rainfall. _____

4. This is a large body of salt water. _____

5. This area is higher than a plain and lower than a mountain. _____

6. This land mass is surrounded by water on three sides. _____

7. This land mass emerges from the water. _____

8. This low-lying area often contains a river. _____

9. This body of water has land on all sides.

_____

Homophone Challenge

Homophones are words that sound the same but have different meanings. Look at each pair of homophones below and see if you can write a sentence that uses both.

1. bald/bawled

The **bald** baby **bawled** when her pacifier fell on the floor.

2. berry/bury

_____

3. capital/capitol

_____

4. feat/feet

_____

5. haul/hall

_____

6. kernel/colonel

_____

7. lesson/lessen

_____

8. mince/mints

_____

9. patience/patients

_____

10. reign/rain

_____

Order Up!

Order the numbers from least to greatest.

1. 6,751   6,075   6,001   6,571

   _____   _____   _____   _____

2. 2,450   2,405   2,045   2,005

   _____   _____   _____   _____

Order the numbers from greatest to least.

3. 3,900   3,390   3,039   3,339

   _____   _____   _____   _____

4. 7,077   7,107   7,707   7,177

   _____   _____   _____   _____

Apply what you know to answer the questions.

5. Joshua has ticket number 37,500. His brother has number 37,502. His sister has number 36,499. If the family bought 4 consecutive tickets, what number does their father have? _____

6. Chase had five business orders fall off his desk. Assist him with putting them in order from least to greatest. The numbers were 987; 1,299; 10,299; 1,001; and 10,001.

   _____

7. Treetop Elementary School served 3,967 hamburgers, 3,566 turkey sandwiches, 3,506 orders of macaroni, and 3,997 slices of pizza. Put the lunches in order from most favorite to the least favorite. _____

So Much Energy!

Read each statement. Decide if the object has potential energy or kinetic energy.
Write *potential* or *kinetic*.

1. A toy car

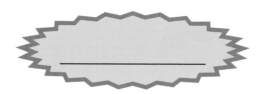

2. A toy car going down
a cardboard ramp

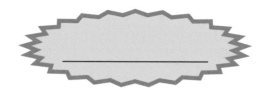

3. A jump rope

4. A girl jumping over a rope

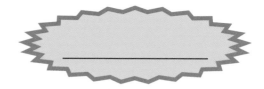

5. A glass of water

6. Water pouring out of a glass

7. A baseball bat

8. A hitter swinging
a baseball bat

Sweet Synonym

Draw a line to match each word with its synonym.

melt	satisfied
appetizing	dissolve
stale	new
fresh	uncooked
plain	burned
raw	nibble
charred	delicious
creamy	spoiled
mix	ordinary
slice	smooth
eat	blend
hungry	cut
full	famished

The Pizza Place

Name the value of the underlined digit.

example: 7<u>5</u>   <u>tens</u>

1. 46<u>8</u> _____

2. 3,6<u>5</u>5 _____

3. <u>4</u>,902 _____

4. 5,<u>5</u>99 _____

5. <u>1</u>0,490 _____

Write a 5 digit number with the given value included.

example: twenty   1<u>5,025</u>

6. six hundred _____

7. four thousand _____

Write a number using the conditions that are given.

example: A two in the thousands place and a three in the tens place   1<u>2,039</u>

8. A one in the hundreds place and a six in the ones place _____

9. A seven in the ten thousands place and a seven in the hundreds place _____

Population Problems

Use the population chart to answer the questions.

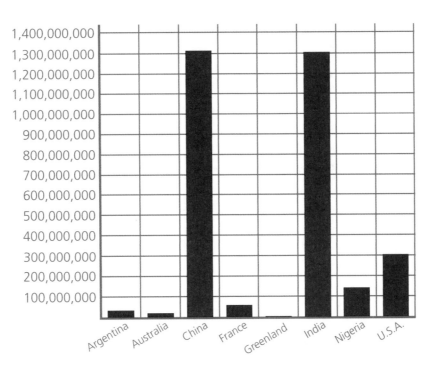

1. What information does this graph give you? _____

2. How many people live in the United States? _____

3. Which country has the lowest population? _____

4. Which country has a smaller population than the United States but a larger population than France? _____

5. Which two countries have more than 1 billion people? _____

   _____

6. What kinds of challenges might India and China face due to the size of their populations? _____

Antonym Apparel

Match each word with its antonym.

outrageous	spend
popular	sensible
light	uncommon
massive	reveal
expensive	inaccurate
silky	frivolous
long	heavy
fitted	dainty
crooked	cheap
functional	straight
precise	loose
cover	short
save	rough

What Goes Around

Round to the nearest given place value.

1. The Ferris Wheel at the County Fair makes 1,675 rotations in a day.

Round to the tens _____

Round to the hundreds _____

Round to the thousands _____

2. The exact number of light bulbs on the Ferris Wheel is 9,806.

Round to the tens _____

Round to the hundreds _____

Round to the thousands _____

3. The County Fair attracts 13,391 people in a day.

Round to the tens _____

Round to the hundreds _____

Round to the thousands _____

4. The total attendance for the fair was 104,362 people. That number is 5,230 more than attended last year. How many people attended the fair last year?

Round to the tens _____

Round to the hundreds _____

Round to the thousands _____

Making Things Go

People use the energy provided by nature to help them do work. For example, they construct mills that use the power of wind to grind grain. Manmade dams harness waterpower to create electric energy. Solar energy can be used to power everything from pocket calculators to spaceships. Wind, water, and the sun are all sources of renewable energy. They are resources that will never run out.

Answer the questions about the reading.

1. Describe one way that people use wind, water, or solar power to help them do work.

_____

_____

2. What is one advantage to using these resources?_____

_____

3. Imagine that you are a member of the Natural Energy Foundation, a group that promotes the use of wind, water, and solar power. Design a poster to encourage people to use these renewable sources of energy.

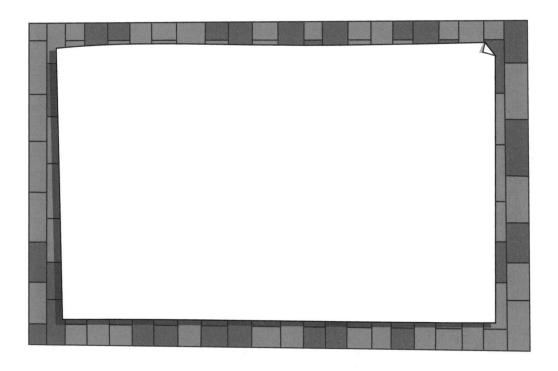

Interpret an Idiom

An idiom is an expression whose meaning does not match the words in the phrase. If someone is called "a babe in the woods," it does not mean he or she is a baby who was left in the forest. Instead, it means he or she is inexperienced.

Write the meaning of each idiom. Then use it in a sentence.

1. a fish out of water _____

_____

2. a penny for your thoughts _____

_____

3. all your eggs in one basket _____

_____

4. back to square one _____

_____

5. butterflies in your stomach _____

_____

6. open a can of worms _____

_____

7. under the weather _____

_____

It's in The Stars

Round each number to the given place value.

1. The distance from Earth to the moon is 384,403 km.

Round to the nearest 10 _____

Round to the nearest 100 _____

Round to the nearest 1,000 _____

Round to the nearest 10,000 _____

Round to the nearest 100,000 _____

2. The number of asteroids in our solar system is 376,537.

Round to the nearest 10 _____

Round to the nearest 100 _____

Round to the nearest 1,000 _____

Round to the nearest 10,000 _____

Round to the nearest 100,000 _____

3. The diameter of the moon is 11,404,800 ft.

Round to the nearest 10 _____

Round to the nearest 100 _____

Round to the nearest 1,000 _____

Round to the nearest 10,000 _____

Round to the nearest 100,000 _____

The People's Property

Identify a human-made feature in your community, such as a road, bridge, building, track, or canal.

Draw a picture of it.

Explain how that human-made feature has helped or hurt your community.

_____

_____

_____

_____

_____

_____

Hear the Homophones

Read each word. Write its homophone.

1. air	heir
2. band	
3. chute	
4. doe	
5. ant	
6. idle	
7. pole	
8. rung	
9. ate	
10. bored	
11. chord	
12. dear	
13. die	
14. mite	
15. meddle	
16. not	
17. days	
18. creek	

Close Enough

Answer each question with either an exact answer or an estimate. Explain your answer.

1. There were 81,596 visitors to the Art Museum last year. Next year the visitors are expected to double. If you were planning for next year, would you use an exact number or an estimate? _____

2. A concession stand had 47 postcards left from the last order when the new order arrived with 144 additional cards. About how many do they have now? If they usually sell about 150 postcards a week, do they have enough for the week?

_____

_____

3. Tour guides can take up to 13 people on a tour. If they give two tours before lunch, about how many people have they served? _____

_____

4. A painting is bought for the collection. The price was $2,457,900. The tax was $196,632. What amount should appear on the check to the seller of the painting?_____

_____

5. An insurance company needs to know how many paintings and how many sculptures are in the museum. There are 671 art pieces in the museum. There are 135 sculptures, 97 statues, and the rest are paintings. What should the response to the insurance company be? _____

_____

6. When budgeting for future additions to the art collection, the museum plans to save a portion of the income from the ticket sales. If they save one fourth of the $807,556 in ticket sales, about how much will they have? _____

_____

What a Wave

Complete the following steps to conduct the experiment. Answer the follow-up questions.

Step 1: Fill a large tub with water.

Step 2: Place a lightweight object on the surface of the water. It should float easily. Try using a ping-pong ball, a rubber duck, or plastic toy boat.

Step 3: Find a rock or other object that will easily sink.

Step 4: Wait until the water in the tub is still.

Step 5: Drop the heavy object into the tub.

Step 6: Carefully observe what happens to the surface of the water and the lightweight object still floating on top.

Step 7: Write your observations down or take a digital photograph or video.

1. What happened to the lightweight object when the water was still?

_____

2. What happened to the surface of the water when you dropped in the heavy object?

_____

3. What happened to the lightweight object when you dropped in the heavy object?

_____

4. Why do you think that happened? _____

_____

5. How does wave energy affect objects? _____

_____

A Wound Up Wound

A homograph is a word that has two completely different meaning and often two different pronounciations. Write a sentence for each homograph that uses both of its meanings. Draw an illustration of your favorite sentence.

wound ___The nurse wound a bandage around the wound.___

1. lie _____

2. tear _____

3. fair _____

4. lead _____

5. bow _____

6. dove _____

Expanding Your Possibilities

Use your knowledge of expanded notation.

1. Write the number 536 in expanded form.

    _____ + _____ + _____

2. Saul has $793 in his saving account. Write Saul's balance in expanded notation.

    _____ + _____ + _____

3. Leah has four hundred dollar bills, four ten dollar bills, and one one dollar bill. How much does she have total? Write in expanded notation.

    _____ + _____ + _____ = _____

4. Ming sold her bike and received two hundred dollar bills, and nine one dollar bills. How much did she sell the bike for? Write in expanded form.

    _____ + _____ = _____

5. The city block measures 1,580 feet. How can you write that in expanded form?

    _____ + _____ + _____ + _____

6. Hakim is asked to write a 3 digit number that uses the same digit in each place value. Using expanded notation, what is a possible answer Hakim might give?

    _____ + _____ + _____ = _____

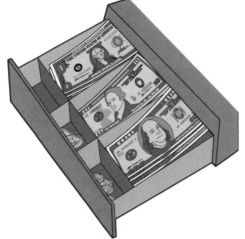

Save the Earth

Natural resources are things in nature that people use, such as water, trees, and land. People use natural resources in many different ways. How humans use the natural resources affects how many resources we will have available later on.

Use what you learned from the reading to fill in the blanks.

1. Brainstorm a list of ways people use natural resources.

_____

_____

_____

2. Brainstorm ways people can conserve natural resources.

_____

_____

_____

3. On a separate piece of paper, write an article for the opinions page of your local newspaper. Encourage people to conserve natural resources. Include some of the ideas you brainstormed above.

FAST FACT	Did you know that 25 billon gallons of water are used in the state of California each day? How many gallons of water do you use each day?

Prefix Puzzle

Match the puzzle pieces.

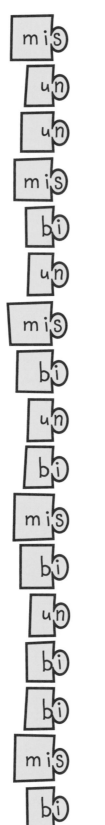

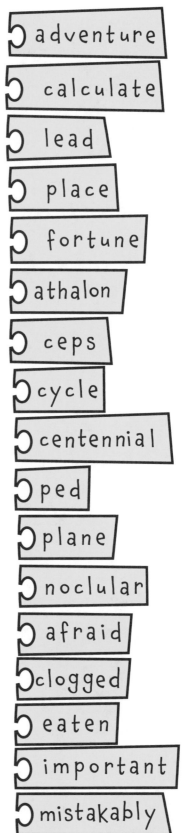

That's Electrifying

Electric devices must be connected to an energy source to use electricity. Electric energy flows from the device to the power source and back again along a path called an electric circuit. Some simple circuits have switches that let you stop and start the flow of electricity. When the switch is open, a space separates the wires of the circuit, stopping the electric current.

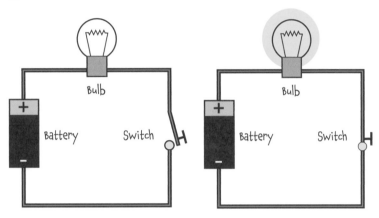

Using what you have learned about electric currents, write a short paragraph explaining how a flashlight works.

_____

_____

_____

_____

_____

_____

_____

_____

The Positive and the Negative

Numbers or integers that are less than zero are called negative. Any number greater than zero is positive. Zero is neither negative nor positive. Use this information to answer the questions below.

1. On the above number line, any number to the left of 0 is _____.

2. On the above number line, any number to the right of 0 is _____.

3. If you put your finger on −1, how many spaces to the right is 0?_____

4. Put your finger on −2. How many spaces to the right is +2? _____

5. Begin on +4 and count to the left until you land on −3. How many spaces did you count? _____

Use the thermometer to answer the questions below.

6. Right now, the temperature is 8° F. If the temperature drops 9° tonight, how cold will it be in the morning? _____

7. At 10 AM, the thermometer read −2°F. By noon, it had risen 10°. What was the temperature at noon? _____

8. Sherwin started ice skating on the pond at 4 PM. The temperature was 12°F. Thirty minutes later, it had dropped 10°. What was the temperature? _____

9. The coldest place on earth is Vostok, Antarctica with a record setting temperature of −129° F. What is the temperature in your town today? What is the difference?_____

Guess the Suffixes

The suffix –er and –or indicate a person who does something. Write a word using the correct suffix.

1. I am a person who types on a computer. I create stories that people like to read. Who am I? _____

2. I am a person who takes care of a garden. I tend to the plants and other living things. Who am I? _____

3. I am a person who pretends to be someone else. I work on stage or in film. Who am I? _____

4. I am a person who helps people learn. I usually work in a classroom. Who am I?

_____

5. I am a person who helps people get well. I often wear a white coat. Who am I?

_____

6. I am a person who rides waves in the ocean. I use a long, flat board to ride. Who am I? _____

7. Now write your own riddles.

_____

_____

_____

_____

_____

_____

_____

_____

"Sum" Heavy Addition

Find the sum.

1. 3,560
   + 4,210

2. 27,813
   + 15,799

3. 67,549
   + 43,612

4. 35,100
   + 9,256

5. 76,890
   + 10,089

6. 99,457
   +   543

The Rammel School is adding on to their campus. The work will require many deliveries of materials and supplies. Help keep track of the inventory. Write a problem and solve it.

7. There were two deliveries of lumber in June. The first carried 16,750 feet of lumber, the second had 2,000 feet of lumber. What is the total?

_____

8. The first cement delivery that month was 31,500 pounds. The second delivery was 24,680 pounds. How much cement was delivered?

_____

9. The number of nails and fasteners needed in the first half of the month was 52,890. The second half of the month required 45,990. How many fasteners and nails were used in that month alone?

_____

10. The cost to furnish the first floor of the school building was $41,324. The second floor is going to cost $39,005. What is the total cost of furnishings?

_____

Native American Cultures

On this page and the next, read the selections about three different tribes.

The Wampanoag Indians

The Wampanoag Indian tribe enjoyed a traditional life of farming, hunting and gathering, and fishing on the land now known as New England. The tribe organized itself into smaller groups. Each group had its own leader called a sachem. The sachem was responsible for leading his own group, but there was no chief of the tribe. The tribe had its own spoken language and unique customs.

In 1620, the Wampanoag had their first contact with European settlers. English Pilgrims settled in Plymouth Colony on Wampanoag land. In 1621, the Wampanoag Indians made a treaty with the Pilgrims. The Pilgrims agreed to protect the Wampanoag from other tribes and the Wampanoag agreed not to attack the settlers. They celebrated this agreement with a feast that has been called the First Thanksgiving.

The relationship with the European settlers was not completely positive. The contact with Europeans introduced many diseases to the Native Americans. The Wampanoag did not have resistance to these diseases and many of them died from smallpox, measles, and other illnesses. In addition, the settlers continued to take over land and eventually went to war with the Wampanoag in 1676. The Wampanoag lost the war and European settlers dominated the region for many years.

The Iroquois Indians

The Iroquois Indians had perhaps the most well organized tribe in North America. Centered in what is now New York state, they formed a federation of five nations: the Mohawk, Oneida, Onondaga, Cayuga, and Seneca. All the tribes were represented and made decisions together. Women were very important in the tribe. Females decided who to nominate for the tribal council and when they needed to be removed if they failed to perform justly.

The Iroquois Indians developed their own spoken language and constructed elaborate longhouses. They were farmers planting corn, beans, and squash. They hunted and were celebrated warriors. They used their own weapons and learned to use European weapons skillfully. With that advantage, the Iroquois were able to take over the neighboring tribes along the Atlantic coast. Many historians believe the Iroquois Indians played a deciding role in the war between the British and the French in 1754. They sided with the British and the British won!

The Cherokee Indians

Before European settlers arrived in North America, the Cherokee Indians lived near the Appalachian Mountains in the southeast. They farmed and hunted and they developed a very sophisticated culture and government structure.

The Cherokee Indians formed a tribal government that resembled European governments. They created a representative system in which various groups were represented at the tribal council. They created different levels of government with specific roles and tasks to perform. The Cherokee also quickly adapted to European economics. They traded shrewdly and owned plantations. In the 1800s, a Cherokee named Sequoyah introduced writing to record the Cherokee legacy and language.

The Cherokee Indians suffered at the hands of Europeans. In 1839, thousands of Cherokee were forced to leave their territory in the southeastern United States. The U.S. military forced them to walk the "Trail of Tears" to what is now Oklahoma. Thousands of Native Americans died along the way. However, the Cherokee were resilient. They reestablished their nation and built schools. Today, the Cherokee Nation has the greatest population of any Native American tribe in the United States.

Show What You Know

Now that you have read about three different Native American cultures, it's time to do some research of your own. First, find out what Native American tribes lived in your area. Then write a short report about these people. Tell what they ate and how they lived. Discuss their form of government and any important details about their culture that you find interesting.

_____

_____

_____

_____

_____

_____

_____

_____

_____

_____

_____

_____

_____

_____

_____

Play with Words

Use a thesaurus to find a synonym and antonym for each word.

	SYNONYM	ANTONYM
locate		
expand		
sturdy		
inaudible		
probable		
frugal		
regular		
dingy		

What a Big Difference!

Solve.

1. 3,736
    − 125

2. 4,225
    − 575

3. 21,341
    − 677

4. 86,021
    − 9,249

5. 51,663
    − 49,554

6. 77,146
    − 19,150

7. 42,670
    − 19,231

8. 125,699
    − 99,038

9. 67,981
    − 25,903

Find the difference.

10. Magnet Enterprises manufactured 70,342 magnets last year. They sold 67,300 magnets to office supply stores. How many magnets are left in their warehouse?

_____

11. The same company sells magnet boards. They made 31,420 boards and shipped 20,144 to customers. How many are left in the inventory?

_____

12. Magnet Enterprises made $91,987 on the magnet boards. The cost to produce them is $1.00 a piece. If they sold 20,144 boards, how much profit did they make?

_____

13. A strong box is required to ship these items. Magnet Enterprises ordered 43,000 boxes but only received 39,670 boxes. How many are missing?

_____

What's the Matter?

Look at each graphic organizer. Read the clues. Guess what the object is.
Tell whether the object is a solid, a liquid, or a gas.
Write your answers in each graphic organizer.

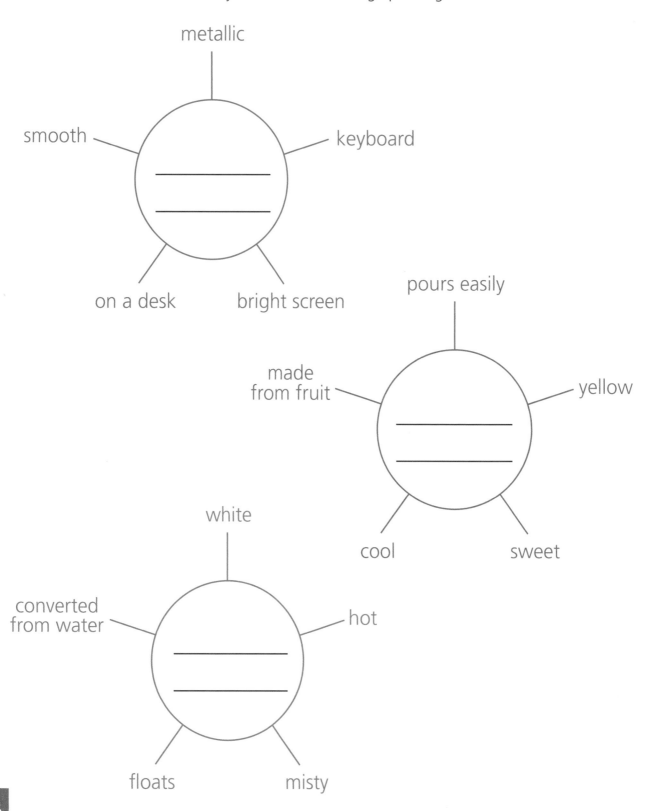

metallic

smooth — keyboard

on a desk — bright screen

pours easily

made from fruit — yellow

cool — sweet

white

converted from water — hot

floats — misty

Our New Neighbors

The moving truck pulled onto our street this morning. It was gigantic and rumbled loudly down the road. We watched from the front porch as the truck stopped at the house across the street. Four men jumped out of the truck and whipped open the back gate. They began unloading heavy boxes and massive amounts of furniture.

A little while later, a car maneuvered its way up to the house. Kids spilled out of the back of the car like little ants scurrying away toward their home. They shouted and laughed as they ran to the front door. We wondered how many kids there were. Would any of them want to play with us? Would they like to play baseball or listen to music?

Use context clues from the story to define each word.

1. What does the word *rumbled* mean? _____

_____

2. What does the word *massive* mean? _____

_____

3. What does *maneuvered* mean? _____

_____

4. What does *scurrying* mean? _____

_____

Practice Makes Perfect

Cover the right half of the page. Time yourself as you solve the problems on the left. Check your answers, then try the problems on the remaining half. Did your time improve?

First Race			**Second Race**		

$$2 \times 6 \qquad 3 \times 4 \qquad 8 \times 5 \qquad\qquad 7 \times 9 \qquad 1 \times 0 \qquad 6 \times 6$$

$$2 \times 9 \qquad 8 \times 3 \qquad 4 \times 7 \qquad\qquad 7 \times 6 \qquad 5 \times 1 \qquad 7 \times 7$$

$$3 \times 5 \qquad 6 \times 4 \qquad 7 \times 8 \qquad\qquad 2 \times 7 \qquad 8 \times 8 \qquad 9 \times 5$$

$$9 \times 9 \qquad 7 \times 5 \qquad 3 \times 9 \qquad\qquad 8 \times 4 \qquad 6 \times 9 \qquad 7 \times 6$$

$$27 \times 3 \qquad 54 \times 9 \qquad 68 \times 5 \qquad\qquad 73 \times 8 \qquad 40 \times 4 \qquad 93 \times 3$$

$$96 \times 6 \qquad 34 \times 2 \qquad 88 \times 7 \qquad\qquad 29 \times 9 \qquad 76 \times 5 \qquad 82 \times 6$$

$$55 \times 4 \qquad 63 \times 7 \qquad 49 \times 5 \qquad\qquad 37 \times 8 \qquad 19 \times 2 \qquad 28 \times 7$$

Total time: _____   Total score: _____   Total time: _____   Total score: _____

40

First People

The first people to live in North America came to the continent thousands of years ago. Scientists believe the first Native Americans, also called American Indians, traveled from Asia to North America more than 15,000 years ago. At that time, sheets of ice covered much of the northern hemisphere. What we know as the northern part of the Pacific Ocean, or the Bering Strait, was actually solid land. This allowed humans to follow the animals they hunted and walk onto the new continent.

Native Americans spread throughout North America and down into South America. Groups separated and formed their own communities with unique cultures. Each tribe spoke its own language, developed its own way of life, and created its own customs. Some tribes lived in villages and farmed. Others built large elaborate cities with sophisticated government systems.

When Europeans arrived in the Americas, Native American life began to disappear. Native Americans were badly affected by the Europeans in many ways. Settlers believed their way of living was better and tried to force the Native Americans to give up their culture. The Europeans also exposed the native people to new diseases like smallpox and measles that killed thousands. Finally, the Europeans fiercely fought Native Americans for land across North and South America.

Answer the questions about the reading.

1. How did Native Americans arrive in North America? _____

_____

2. Describe two different types of cultures that evolved. _____

_____

3. How were Native Americans affected by the arrival of Europeans?_____

_____

_____

The Dictionary

Place each word from the word bank in the correct place on the dictionary page.
Write a brief definition for each word.

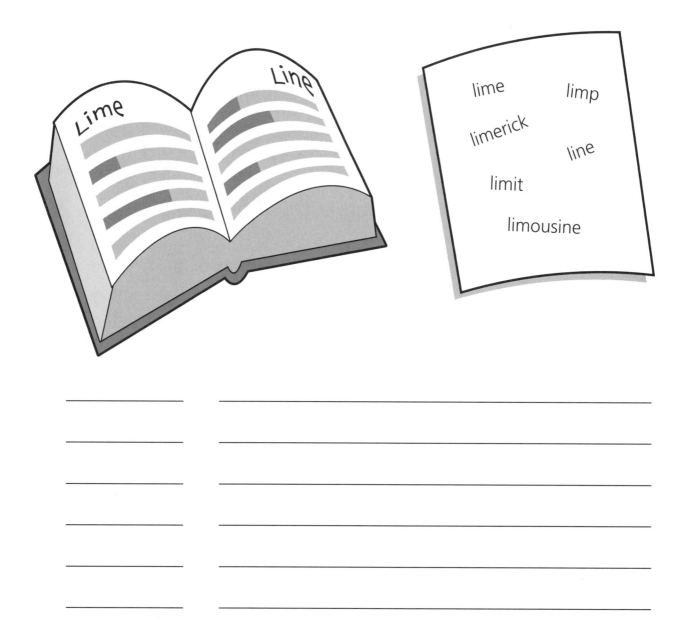

lime   limp

limerick

limit   line

limousine

_____   _____

_____   _____

_____   _____

_____   _____

_____   _____

ON YOUR OWN   Write a story using all of the words in this activity.
Share your story with friends and family.

Check It Out

Inverse operations can be used to check your work. The inverse of multiplication is division.
Solve each problem. Then use the inverse operation to check your work.

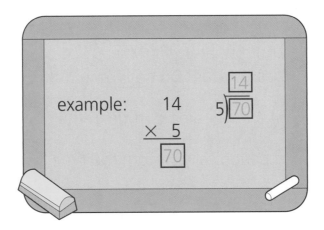

example: 14
            × 5
           70

5)70
14

1.   19
       × 6

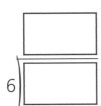

6)

2.   230
       × 8

8)

3.   52
       × 9

9)

4.

3)75

× 3

5.

9)333

× 9

6.

7)616

× 7

Summer Science Fun

Try these two simple experiments on a hot, sunny day. Record your observations and results.

Experiment 1

Step 1: Find two socks. Get them both very wet. Wring out one sock and squeeze out as much water as you can. Do not wring out the other sock.

Step 2: Hang both socks on a clothesline outside in the sun.

Step 3: Observe both socks periodically. Record the time and what you observe.

Step 4: When one sock is dry, record how long it took for that sock to dry. Record what you observe about the second sock.

1. Which sock dried first?_____

2. Why do you think that sock dried first? _____

_____

Experiment 2

Step 1: Find a small piece of chocolate. Unwrap it and place it on a plate in direct sunlight.

Step 2: Start a stopwatch or timer.

Step 3: Observe the piece of chocolate every three minutes. Record the time and your observations.

Step 4: When the chocolate has completely melted, stop the timer or stopwatch. Record the time.

1. How long did it take for the chocolate to melt? _____

2. How did the chocolate change from a solid to a liquid?_____

_____

Word Play

Words can have more than one meaning. Look at some examples:

I've got a beef with the beef the butcher gave me.

Jake pounds a pound of dough into a round ball.

Write a sentence for each word that uses both of its meanings.

tap	angle	dash	deck
bowl	might	wind	bear

1. _____

2. _____

3. _____

4. _____

5. _____

6. _____

7. _____

8. _____

It's Elementary

Solve each problem.

1. In the first grade at Oceanview Elementary, there are 125 students. Each student uses 5 pencils. How many pencils should the school order? _____

2. There are 625 students in each grade. The school includes grades 1 to 6. If each student is provided a school t-shirt, how many shirts are needed? _____

3. The students had a fundraiser to plant new trees at the school. Each of the 317 students that participated sold 5 tickets each. How many tickets were sold?

_____

4. The principal's birthday is celebrated each year. There are 9 classes with 27 students in each class. How many cupcakes does the principal need to bake to give one to each student? _____

5. For the first day of school each entrance is decorated with balloons. There are 124 balloons at each of the 4 entrances. How many are there in all? _____

6. Every grade uses at least 1,568 pieces of paper per week. If there are 6 grades at the school, how many sheets of paper are used each week? _____

7. There are 87 books on each shelf of the library. In the upper grades reading section, there are 25 shelves of books. How many books are available for the upper grade students to read? _____

8. In the cafeteria, lunch is served to 625 students each day. Lunch is served 5 days a week. If there are 4 weeks in a month, how many lunches are served each month at Oceanview Elementary? _____

Local Life

Every town has something special to offer. Maybe your town offers beautiful architecture or special cuisine. Maybe it's the home of a famous historical event or the birthplace of an important person. Maybe it's just a great place to live!

Pretend you work in your town's tourism office. It's your job to create a brochure inviting visitors to your town. Write about what makes your town unique. If possible, use the Internet to add important facts to your writing, including the date your town was founded and its current population. Remember to add as many colorful descriptive words as you can to your writing in order to make your brochure—and your town—as interesting as possible. Add a picture to your brochure to give it extra appeal.

ON YOUR OWN   Design a poster to go with your brochure.

Teeth-chattering Tundra

The Arctic is the northernmost part of planet Earth. It is a tundra, or frozen plain, where the sun never rises above the horizon in winter. Plants that live in the Arctic have had to adapt to the harsh climate. Since the growing season is so short, plants have developed unique ways of growing. They have elaborate root systems that are able to extract the scarce nutrients from the harsh soil. Arctic plants also have the ability to remain alive under the thick blanket of snow in the winter. As soon as the snow melts, the plants are ready to grow!

Animals in the Arctic have special adaptations as well. Herbivores often leave the area during the winter months when plants are not available. Predators either migrate, following prey to warmer areas, or hibernate. Animals that stay in the frozen tundra usually live off the fat stored in their bodies. Musk oxen restrict activity to conserve their body heat, while foxes and wolves grow thick winter fur to keep them warm. Other animals, such as squirrels, burrow underground to wait out the cold season.

Circle the best answer to each question.

1. Which is the correct definition of *tundra*?

a. the northernmost part of Earth
b. the North Pole
c. a frozen plain

2. Which one is an adaptation of plants in the Arctic?

a. elaborate root systems
b. migration to warmer climates
c. limited sunshine

3. How have wolves adapted to living in the Arctic?

a. restrict activity during cold season
b. hibernate in underground caves
c. grow thick fur

4. Which sentence most clearly tells what this passage is mostly about?

a. The Arctic is the northernmost part of planet Earth.
b. Plants and animals that live in the Arctic have had to adapt to the harsh climate.
c. The Arctic is a tundra, and there is not a wide variety of plant life.

Getting Groceries

Find the quotient.

1. There are 146 shopping carts at the grocery store. If they are divided between the 2 entrances, how many carts are at each entrance? _____

2. On the 3 shelves of cereal, there are 642 boxes stocked. How many boxes are on each shelf? _____

3. The baker made 144 cookies at 5:00 AM. They are packaged into boxes of 6. How many boxes of cookies are there? _____

4. The 7 main departments of the market are produce, dairy, dry goods, meat, frozen food, beverages, and seasonal merchandise. These areas take up 8,673 square feet of floor space. About how much area is designated to each space?

   _____

5. In a week, 6,195 pounds of meat are sold to the customers. If equal parts of chicken, beef, pork, turkey, and fish are sold, how much of each kind of meat is sold? _____

6. Approximately 2,452 bags are used by customers every day. The average shopper uses 4 bags. How many shoppers take their groceries in bags each day?

   _____

7. Over a 3 month period, there were 831 suppliers making deliveries to the store. About how many deliveries are made in 1 month?

   _____

8. Using 1,000 bananas, make a division problem that has no remainder.

   _____

   _____

Kitchen Science

1. Place a cup of sugar on the table. Describe the properties of the sugar.

_____

_____

_____

_____

2. Place a cup of butter on the table. Describe the properties of the butter.

_____

_____

_____

_____

3. Using an electric mixer (with an adult's permission), blend the two substances together for two minutes. Describe the properties of the mixture.

_____

_____

_____

_____

Summer Fun

Read each passage. Then answer the question.

There are some important things you should do before you roller skate for the first time. First, find skates that fit you properly. They shouldn't be so big that your feet slide around inside. Next, strap on protective gear. Wear a helmet that fits your head and wrist pads to protect your hands and wrists. Put on elbow and knee pads so they fit snugly. Finally, you should start slowly. Stand up on the skates and get comfortable with the feeling of being on wheels. It is slippery! Try shuffling your feet a little so you can feel what it is like when the wheels move. Then take a small step forward. You are ready to skate!

1. What are the three important things to do before roller skating for the first time?

_____

_____

_____

The sun is especially strong during the summer months. It is important to protect your skin from the harmful rays of the sun. You can protect yourself in a couple of ways. First, wear a hat when you are outside. It will protect your face and scalp from the burning rays of the sun. It will also shield your eyes from the sun. It is also crucial to wear sunscreen. Slather the protective cream over your skin any time you go outdoors. You should put on sun protection every day. It will help protect you from burning your skin. Reapply sunscreen if you are swimming or sweating!

2. What are two ways you can protect your skin from the sun?

_____

_____

Nuts and Bolts of 1 and 0

The numbers 1 and 0 have unique properties. Answer the questions.

1. Illustrate 5 multiplied by 1. Write an equation._____

2. Illustrate 9 divided by 1. Write an equation. _____

3. How are these two equations similar?

_____

_____

4. If you multiply a number by 0, what is the product? Explain how this is so.

_____

_____

5. Can you divide a given number into "no groups"?

_____

_____

6. Can you divide "nothing" into groups? How many in each group?

_____

_____

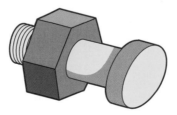

Super Citizens

Brainstorm some ideas about how good citizens behave at school, in your community, and in our country. List your ideas in the columns below.

SCHOOL	COMMUNITY	COUNTRY

What citizenship behaviors are common in school, in the community, and in the country? _____

_____

ON YOUR OWN	Design an award for good citizenship. It can be a ribbon, certificate, or trophy. Create your award from paper or other art supplies. Give the award to someone you know who deserves it.

Predict the Future

Read each sentence. Write your prediction about what will happen next.
Explain why you think that will happen.

1. The empty milk carton is in the refrigerator. Dad pours a bowl of cereal. He reaches into the refrigerator for the milk.

_____

_____

_____

2. Jenetta studies hard for her language arts test. She reads all the books the teacher recommends. Jenetta sits down to take the test on Friday.

_____

_____

_____

3. The sky looks gray. Dark clouds block the sunlight. Mrs. Logan's class is preparing for their Spring Picnic. They set up tables outside on the playground.

_____

_____

_____

ON YOUR OWN

Write a story using one of the prompts on this page. Include your prediction as part of the story. Illustrate your story and share it with your family.

Arcade Abundance

Troy's Toys buys boxes of each toy. Solve to find out the cost per item.

ITEM	TOTAL COST	NUMBER OF UNITS	UNIT COST
1. Bouncy balls	$4.95	9	
2. Yo-yos	$3.60	3	
3. Hula Hoops	$14.40	4	
4. Jacks	$11.52	6	
5. Rings	$1.61	7	
6. Flying Discs	$6.58	2	
7. Star Glasses	$24.72	8	
8. Temporary Tattoos	$0.45	5	
9. Kazoo	$3.99	1	
10. Jump ropes	$41.85	9	

All About Atoms

Fill in the surrounding circles with what you know about atoms.
Use the Internet or other resources to help you.

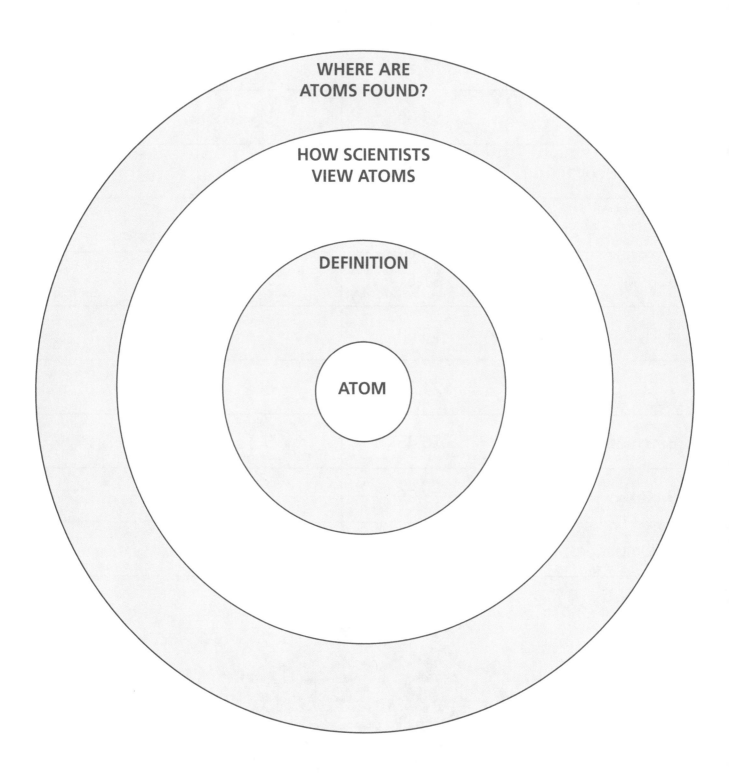

WHERE ARE
ATOMS FOUND?

HOW SCIENTISTS
VIEW ATOMS

DEFINITION

ATOM

Famous Female Native Americans

Pocahontas was the daughter of a Powhatan leader. She was an influential person in the relationship between Native Americans and Europeans. There is a famous story about Pocahontas saving the life of a settler named John Smith. Historians are not sure if the story is true. Pocahontas did eventually marry an English settler named John Rolfe. She worked hard to improve the relationship between Europeans and Native Americans.

Sacagawea was a Shoshone Indian who helped Lewis and Clark on their expedition across North America. She joined the explorers in North Dakota. Since Sacagawea was married to a French-Canadian man, she had connections to both Native Americans and Europeans. Lewis and Clark recognized how she might be able to help them talk with other native people they met. When the explorers met with Shoshone Indians in the Rocky Mountains, Sacagawea helped secure horses for the trip and negotiated peaceful passage. She was very helpful throughout the trip across the Northwest.

Answer the questions about the reading.

1. What could be another title for this passage? _____

2. What is the main idea for paragraph 1? _____

_____

3. What are two supporting details from paragraph 1? _____

_____

4. What is the main idea of paragraph 2? _____

_____

5. What are two supporting details from paragraph 2? _____

_____

Piece of Cake

Equivalent fractions are equal. Color the second fraction
in each pair to see how the two fractions are equivalent.

1. $\frac{1}{2}$  $\frac{4}{8}$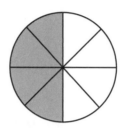

2. $\frac{4}{16}$ 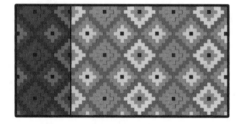 $\frac{1}{4}$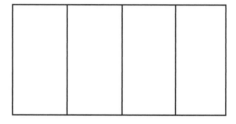

3. $\frac{3}{9}$  $\frac{1}{3}$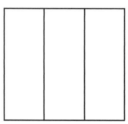

4. $\frac{9}{12}$  $\frac{3}{4}$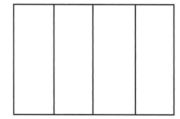

The American Flag

The first flag of the United States was created in 1777. The Continental Congress passed the first Flag Act to make it a symbol of the new country. The Continental Congress decided the flag would have thirteen red and white stripes and thirteen white stars on a blue field. As each new state joined the union, a star was added to the blue field. Today, the flag contains 50 stars and 13 stripes.

Everything about the flag is symbolic. Red symbolizes bravery. White stands for purity. Blue represents perseverance and justice. Stars often symbolize divine goals to which humans have always aspired. The stripes mimic the rays of light coming from the sun.

There are rules about how to display and use the flag. The flag must never touch the ground. It should be lighted at all times by sunlight or an artificial light source. A flag that is flown upside down is a signal of distress. Flags must be neatly folded when they are stored. A flag is an important symbol of any country and should be treated with respect and dignity.

Answer the questions about the readings.

1. Why do you think a flag is an important symbol? _____

_____

2. Why do you think the Founding Fathers selected red, white, and blue as the colors for the flag? How do the colors symbolize the values of the United States?

_____

_____

3. Make an argument for changing the colors of the flag. Support your argument with details and facts. _____

_____

_____

_____

That's a Problem

Underline the problem in each passage. Provide a possible solution.

1. Jorge was riding his bike to the park. He was pedaling as fast as he could. Suddenly, his shoelace got caught in the chain.

_____

2. Celina wanted to bake cupcakes. She had flour, sugar, and eggs. She didn't have any milk.

_____

3. Ethan and Hank were camping. They set up the tent. They rolled out their sleeping bags. They started to build a fire. They didn't have any matches to light the fire.

_____

4. Marco picked 47 lemons from the tree. Wendy picked 25 lemons from the tree. They needed to get the lemons to Pedro's house in one hour for the lemonade stand.

_____

5. Zoe put on her helmet and strapped on her pads. She carried her skateboard down the driveway to the sidewalk. As she put the board down, she noticed the neighbor's dog running off down the street without his owner.

_____

Daily Dose of Fractions

Solve each problem and write the answer in simplest form.

1. Ingrid wanted to double her favorite pancake recipe. It calls for $\frac{1}{4}$ cup of sugar. How much sugar will she need if she doubles that amount? _____

2. The cookie dough needed to chill in the refrigerator for $\frac{1}{3}$ of an hour and then rest at room temp for $\frac{2}{3}$ of an hour. How long will it take to prepare the dough?

_____

3. The right fielder scored $\frac{3}{8}$ of the points at the baseball game. The left fielder scored $\frac{2}{8}$ of the team's points. What fraction of the points did they score together?

_____

4. At the basketball game, $\frac{4}{6}$ of the freethrows were scored by the point guard. The center scored $\frac{1}{6}$ of them. What fraction of the freethrows were made by the two of them? _____

5. Students arrive to school in three different ways. Walkers make up $\frac{2}{5}$ of the students, bicyclists are $\frac{1}{5}$, and $\frac{2}{5}$ of the students arrive by car. What fraction of the students are bikers and walkers? _____

6. Jake makes the world a little greener by recycling. Of his recyclables, $\frac{3}{12}$ is aluminum, $\frac{4}{12}$ is glass, and $\frac{5}{12}$ is plastic. What fraction is the aluminum and glass?

_____

7. Vanessa surveyed her class for their favorite sport. Water polo was favored by $\frac{2}{9}$ of the class and swimming by $\frac{2}{9}$. What fraction of the class loves pool sports?

_____

8. Mr. Nguyen asked his class when they do homework. Three-tenths do it right after school. Five-tenths do it right after dinner. Two-tenths leave it for after 8 PM. What fraction of the students do their homework before 8 PM? _____

The Bald Eagle

Use the notes to write a paragraph about this important United States symbol.

bald eagle is a large, powerful, brown bird	unique to the United States
"piebald" means marked with white	symbolizes strength, courage, freedom, and immortality
made national bird in 1782	once an endangered species
image of bald eagle found on Great Seal, President's flag, and one-dollar bill	the Bald Eagle Protection Act has saved it from extinction

_____

_____

_____

_____

_____

_____

_____

_____

_____

_____

_____

Build a Board Game

Imagine you received a new game as a gift. Only someone removed the instructions! How frustrating would it be to try to play the game without knowing what to do? What are the rules? What is the object of the game?

When writing instructions for a board game, it is important to explain the object, or goal, of the game. Make sure all steps of the game are carefully explained. You should also make sure to explain all the rules. Take a look at some games you have at home. Examine the rules and directions.

Create your own board game. Write the directions and rules here on this page. Design a playing board on another piece of paper. Invite a friend to play the game with you!

_____

_____

_____

_____

_____

_____

_____

_____

_____

_____

_____

Fraction Fun

Solve each problem and write the answer in simplest form.

1. Jane's birthday cake had 12 slices. She ate one slice and gave a slice to each of the 5 people in her family. What fraction of the cake was left? _____

2. Martin walked his dog for $\frac{1}{6}$ of an hour. He walked his neighbor's dogs for $\frac{2}{6}$ of an hour. How much longer did he spend walking his neighbor's dogs?

_____

3. Alma listens to rock music $\frac{7}{9}$ of the time she is working out. She listens to classical for her cool down $\frac{1}{9}$ of the time. How much more time is spent listening to rock than classical? _____

4. At the Thompsons' barbeque, $\frac{5}{12}$ of the guests ate hot dogs. The Thompsons served hamburgers to $\frac{4}{12}$ of the guests. What fraction of the guests ate neither hot dogs nor hamburgers? _____

5. Victor surveyed the favorite desserts of his whole family. He found that $\frac{2}{3}$ prefer cake, $\frac{1}{6}$ prefer pie, and $\frac{1}{6}$ prefer ice cream. What fraction of people do not prefer ice cream? _____

6. Beach visitors eat many delicious snacks. Two-thirds of the people bring salty snacks. One-third of the people bring sweet fruit. How many more people bring salty snacks than fruit? _____

7. Miss Lee's dancing school offers tap, jazz, and ballet classes. One-third of the students take tap classes. One-third take jazz. What fraction of the students take ballet? _____

8. Drew is almost always running late! He is late to school $\frac{4}{5}$ of the week. What fraction of the week is he on time?

_____

The Statue of Liberty

The Statue of Liberty is located in New York on an island in the middle of New York Harbor. The statue is a widely recognized symbol of freedom all over the world. Its light of freedom welcomed immigrants to the United States through Ellis Island. It remains an important symbol of liberty, freedom, and opportunity in America.

Answer the questions about the reading.

1. List 2 statues that honor people or countries.

_____   _____

2. Why are statues used to honor people or countries or events?

_____

_____

3. Create your own statue. Draw a sketch on another piece of paper. What or who does your statue symbolize? Why did you choose this symbol?

_____

_____

_____

ON YOUR OWN	Make your own statue! Using clay, sculpt the symbol you created in this activity. Share your creation with friends and family. Describe why you chose this symbol and how you completed the project.

A Thrilling Ride

SALLY RIDE

Sally Ride was the first American female astronaut to travel into space. She rode aboard the space shuttle *Challenger* in 1983.

Ride's Early Life

Sally Ride was born in Los Angeles on May 26, 1951. After graduating from Westlake High School in 1968, Ride went to Stanford University in California. She earned her undergraduate degrees and doctorate degree from Stanford.

Sally Ride was the first American female to travel in space.

Ride as an Astronaut

In 1979 Sally Ride completed a one-year training to qualify for space travel. On June 18, 1983 the space shuttle *Challenger* was launched from Kennedy Space Center in Florida. Sally Ride was on board as a mission specialist. During the mission, the crew deployed satellites and conducted scientific experiments.

---

1. What is the title of this chapter? _____

2. What is the first subheading? _____

3. What can you expect to learn from the section called "Ride as an Astronaut"?

_____

4. What is the caption for the picture on the page? _____

_____

Keep It Simple

Solve the problems and write the answer in simplest form.

Example: $\frac{1}{8} + \frac{3}{8} = \frac{4}{8} = \frac{1}{2}$

1. $\frac{1}{2} + \frac{1}{2} =$ _____ = _____

2. $\frac{1}{3} + \frac{1}{3} =$ _____ = _____

3. $\frac{3}{4} - \frac{1}{4} =$ _____ = _____

4. $\frac{7}{8} - \frac{3}{8} =$ _____ = _____

5. $\frac{3}{6} + \frac{1}{6} =$ _____ = _____

6. $\frac{5}{8} - \frac{3}{8} =$ _____ = _____

7. $\frac{2}{12} + \frac{1}{12} =$ _____ = _____

8. $\frac{3}{10} + \frac{2}{10} =$ _____ = _____

9. $\frac{5}{5} - \frac{0}{5} =$ _____ = _____

10. $\frac{3}{12} + \frac{3}{12} =$ _____ = _____

The Constitutional Convention

In 1787, the United States of America was a brand new country. It had just won independence from Great Britain in the Revolutionary War. The young country was busy setting up its government and negotiating problems between the 13 states. Each state wanted its own set of laws. The people in charge of the new United States of America were having a hard time getting all the states to work together and get along.

In May of 1787, 55 men gathered together to find a solution to the problem. They called the meeting the Constitutional Convention. The special delegates met in Independence Hall in Philadelphia. They used their knowledge and experience to make decisions about how to govern the new country. It was very difficult for them to agree. The men had to use discussion and compromise to settle their differences. Eventually, James Madison penned a document called the Constitution of the United States of America.

The Constitution is the set of laws that govern the United States. It explains how the national government works. It also explains all of the laws and rights for the people of the United States. Finally, the Constitution also gives power to each of the states. Each state in the United States has its own set of rules that coincide with the laws of the national government.

Answer the questions about the reading.

1. List four facts you learned about the Constitutional Convention.

_____

_____

_____

2. If you were one of the delegates, what law would you want to include in the Constitution? _____

_____

Causes of Cavities

A cavity is a hole in a tooth. How does a cavity form? When you eat or drink, the food or beverage comes in contact with your teeth. Your saliva helps to break down the food and beverage. Any little bits of food or drink that stay in the mouth stick to your teeth. The bacteria in the food changes into a sticky substance called plaque. The plaque sticks to your teeth and eats away at the enamel on the tooth.

When the plaque stays on your teeth, it will go through the protective enamel of your teeth and put a hole in the tooth. When there is a hole in the tooth, more bacteria can get in the inside the tooth. A cavity must be filled by a dentist or the tooth will start to decay and will eventually die. This can be very painful and can lead to other problems.

Answer the questions about the reading.

1. What causes cavities? _____

2. What happens when little bits of food or drink are left on your teeth?

_____

3. What happens when plaque is left on your teeth? _____

_____

4. What might happen when the tooth decays? _____

_____

Show What You Know

Write a fraction to describe each picture.
Check if the picture shows parts of a whole or parts of a set.

1.

$\dfrac{2}{5}$
_____

_____ Parts of a whole

✓ Parts of a set

2.

_____

_____ Parts of a whole

_____ Parts of a set

3.

_____

_____ Parts of a whole

_____ Parts of a set

4.

_____

_____ Parts of a whole

_____ Parts of a set

5.

_____

_____ Parts of a whole

_____ Parts of a set

6.

_____

_____ Parts of a whole

_____ Parts of a set

The Periodic Table

Look at the Periodic Table of Elements. Answer the questions.

H Hydrogen																	He Helium
Li Lithium	Be Beryllium											B Boron	C Carbon	N Nitrogen	O Oxygen	F Fluorine	Ne Neon
Na Sodium	Mg Magnesium											Al Aluminum	Si Silicon	P Phosphorus	S Sulfur	Cl Chlorine	Ar Argon
K Potassium	Ca Calcium	Sc Scandium	Ti Titanium	V Vanadium	Cr Chromium	Mn Manganese	Fe Iron	Co Cobalt	Ni Nickel	Cu Copper	Zn Zinc	Ga Gallium	Ge Germanium	As Arsenic	Se Selenium	Br Bromine	Kr Krypton
Rb Rubidium	Sr Strontium	Y Ytrium	Zr Zirconium	Nb Niobium	Mo Molybdenum	Tc Technetium	Ru Ruthenium	Rh Rhodium	Pd Palladium	Ag Silver	Cd Cadmium	In Indium	Sn Tin	Sb Antimony	Te Tellurium	I Iodine	Xe Xenon
Cs Cesium	Ba Barium	*	Hf Hafnium	Ta Tantalum	W Tungsten	Re Rhenium	Os Osmium	Ir Iridium	Pt Platinum	Au Gold	Hg Mercury	Tl Thallium	Pb Lead	Bi Bismuth	Po Polonium	At Astatine	Rn Radon
Fr Francium	Ra Radium	**	Rf Unnilquadium	Db Unnilpentium	Sg Unnilhexium	Bh Unnilseptium	Hs Unniloctium	Mt Unnilennium	Uun Unununilium	Uuu Unununium	Uub Ununbium						

	*	La Lanthanum	Ce Cerium	Pr Praseodymium	Nd Neodymium	Pm Promethium	Sm Samarium	Eu Europium	Gd Gadolinium	Tb Terbium	Dy Dysprosium	Ho Holmium	Ho Erbium	Tm Thulium	Yb Ytterbium	Lu Lutetium
	**	Ac Actinium	Th Thorium	Pa Protactinium	U Uranium	Np Neptunium	Pu Plutonium	Am Americium	Cm Curium	Bk Berkelium	Cf Californium	Es Einsteinium	Fm Fermium	Md Mendelevium	No Nobelium	Lr Lawrencium

Element Groups (Families)	Alkalil Earth	Alkaline Earth	Halogens	Metalloids	Noble Gases	Non-Metals	Other Metals	Rare Earth	Transition Metals

1. What information does the Periodic Table give? _____

_____

2. What type of element is magnesium? _____

3. What type of element is silicon? _____

4. What type of element is oxygen? _____

5. How do you think the Periodic Table of Elements is useful to scientists?

_____

_____

Henri Matisse

Henri Matisse was a famous and influential French painter in the early 1900s. He was born December 31, 1869 in Le Cateau, France. As a young man, Matisse moved to Paris to practice and learn more about painting and drawing. He learned to paint with bold brushwork and bright colors. Matisse began to experiment with the effects of light.

From 1904 to 1905, Matisse painted on the coast of the Mediterranean Sea. He was deeply affected by the different light presented in that region. He began to paint more abstractly. When he returned to Paris, he showed his paintings at an art exhibition called the Autumn Salon. The paintings began an art movement called Fauvism. It used vivid colors and flat shapes. Many other artists followed Matisse's style.

Between 1910 and 1912, Matisse spent a lot of time in Spain and Morocco. He was impressed with the Islamic architecture and art. These influences began to appear in Matisse's paintings as colorful objects, textiles, and costumes.

In the later period of his life, Matisse used cutout paper instead of traditional canvas. He cut abstract shapes out of brightly colored paper and grouped them into large-scale compositions.

Place the following facts in sequential order according to the passage.

_____ Matisse painted abstracts on the coast of the Mediterranean Sea.

_____ Matisse used paper cutouts in his art.

_____ Matisse was influenced by Islamic architecture and art.

_____ Matisse experimented with the effects of light.

_____ Matisse moved to Paris as a young man.

_____ Matisse showed his work at the Autumn Salon.

Equal but Different

For every decimal, there is an equivalent fraction. Complete the chart.

	Decimal	Read as	Fraction
1.	.3	three-tenths	$\frac{3}{10}$
2.	.9	nine-tenths	_____
3.	.42	forty-two hundredths	_____
4.	_____	sixty-three hundredths	$\frac{63}{100}$
5.	_____	_____	$\frac{1}{10}$
6.	.91	_____	_____
7.	_____	ten-hundredths	_____
8.	.06	_____	_____
9.	_____	_____	$\frac{9}{100}$
10.	1.0	_____	_____

Common mixed number fractions also have an equivalent decimal. Complete the chart.

	Fraction	Decimal
11.	$1\frac{1}{2}$	1.5
12.	$2\frac{1}{4}$	_____
13.	$\frac{3}{2}$	_____
14.	$1\frac{3}{4}$	_____
15.	$\frac{8}{4}$	_____

Help Wanted

Write a Help Wanted ad for the office of President of the United States.
Include a description of the job responsibilities and qualifications needed.

A Man on the Moon

What you already know about a topic helps you focus when reading.
Think about what you know about space travel and a man named Neil Armstrong.
Write down ten things you already know about these topics.

_____

_____

_____

_____

_____

_____

_____

_____

Write five questions you have about Neil Armstrong. Do some research on the Internet
or in other resources about Neil Armstrong. Find answers to your questions and write
them on a separate sheet of paper.

_____

_____

_____

_____

Fractions All Around Us

Sketch the given fractions.

$\frac{3}{4}$ of a sandwich

$\frac{1}{2}$ of a dozen eggs

$1\frac{2}{3}$ jars of gumballs

$2\frac{1}{4}$ pieces of licorice

$\frac{4}{5}$ of a candy bar

$\frac{3}{8}$ of a pizza

Shadowy Figures

Complete the experiment by following the steps described below.

Step 1: Find an opaque object approximately 12 inches high that can stand on its own, such as a trophy or a small lamp.

Step 2: On a bright, sunny day, take the object outside. You will be repeating the process at two different times of day. Take the object outside at noon and set it on the ground or a table.

Step 3: Observe the shadow cast by the object. Record the time and your observations or take a digital photograph.

Step 4: Mark the spot where you placed the object so you know where to place it next time.

At 6:00 in the evening, take the object back outside. Place it in exactly the same location and position. Record the time and your observations or take a digital photograph.

Answer the questions about your experiment.

1. What did the shadow look like at noon? _____

2. What did the shadow look like at 6:00 PM? _____

3. How are they different? _____

4. What causes a shadow? _____

_____

5. Why were the lengths of the shadows different at different times of the day?

_____

Same or Different?

Choose an animal that interests you. Use two different resources to conduct research on the animal. For example, you might use a nonfiction book and a nature magazine, an encyclopedia and a Web site, or two different animal almanacs. Using the information you gather about the animal from each source, complete the graphic organizer below.

Animal Name:

Title of Resource 1:

Average weight:

Habitat:

Diet:

Interesting fact:

Title of Resource 2:

Average weight:

Habitat:

Diet:

Interesting fact:

How is the information from the two sources similar? _____

_____

_____

How is the information different? _____

_____

_____

Great State

There are 50 states in the United States, and each one is unique. States have their own governments and their own laws. They even have their own flags! Each state's culture, geographical features, and history make it different from its neighbors.

Think about the state where you live. What makes you state special? Answer the questions below. If necessary, use a book or the Internet to help you.

1. My state is located in the _____ part of the United States.

2. The capitol of my state is _____.

3. My state became part of the United States in _____.

4. The main industries in my state are _____.

5. Three words that describe my state are _____.

6. The best thing about my state is _____.

7. If you visit my state, the first thing you place you should go is _____

_____.

Draw a picture that shows a special place, custom, or food that you think represents your state.

Dollars and Cents

Round to the nearest dime.

1. $0.41 _____

2. $0.39 _____

3. $0.25 _____

4. $2.55 _____

5. $9.96 _____

6. $3.93 _____

Round to the nearest dollar.

7. $8.10 _____

8. $16.72 _____

9. $21.50 _____

10. $39.80 _____

11. $99.96 _____

12. $45.45 _____

Complete the chart.

Amount	Round to the nearest dime	Round to the nearest dollar
13. $4.11		
14. $5.79		
15. $5.49		
16. $9.00		
17. $48.75		
18. $199.96		

Oceans of Opinions

Write an opinion about each fact.

1. Sharks have sharp teeth. _____

2. Jellyfish can sting. _____

3. Octopi have eight legs. _____

4. Sea stars can grow new legs. _____

5. Fish have gills. _____

6. Male sea horses carry and protect their eggs. _____

7. Blue whales are the largest animal on earth. _____

8. Turtles can live to be 150 years old. _____

9. Dolphins are mammals. _____

10. Sea slugs are a type of snail. _____

ON YOUR OWN

Write a paragraph expressing your opinion about ocean pollution. Support your opinion with facts.

Vending Machine Madness

Add up the purchases.

1. A bag of chips and candy _____

2. Two sodas _____

3. A sandwich, apple, and water _____

4. Crackers and juice _____

5. Gum and cookies _____

6. Juice and chips _____

A Poem of Light

Below are six facts about light. Read each fact. Then think about what you've learned. Use the facts to write a poem about light. Add as many descriptive words as you can.

Light is a form of energy.

Light you see is visible light.

Color is light energy.

Light is made up of waves that move up and down.

Light travels in a straight line.

Reflection is the way light bounces off an object.

Poem title: _____

_____

_____

_____

_____

_____

_____

_____

_____

_____

_____

Victory for Video Games

What's your favorite video game? You probably know how to play it very well.
Imagine you are going to tell a friend how to play the game. Write detailed instructions
about how to play the video game.

Where Did It All Go?

Solve the problems to figure out how each person spent his or her money.

1. Miguel recycled for three months to earn $74.53. He bought three new CDs for a total of $21.89. How much money is left? _____

2. Sarah babysat her sister to make $100.00. She bought a new mp3 player for $91.00 How much does she still have? _____

3. Frances purchased a bike for $82.00 with the $88.56 she made working and saving. What is the remaining amount? _____

4. Albert washed windows for $25.00 to pay off a debt he owes. If he borrowed $37.00, how much does he still owe? _____

5. Lars spent $135.89 of his $150.00 on a skateboard. What was the change?

_____

6. Collin saved all of his money to buy a car on his sixteenth birthday. He saved $3,156.00. A small sedan was advertised for $3,500.00. How much more money does he need? _____

The Federal System

The United States has a federal system of government. That means there is a set of laws that govern the entire country—called the Constitution of the United States. All 50 states in the United States have to follow the laws of the Constitution.

However, each state also has its own set of laws for the state. That means the state government can make up its own laws unique to the state. So some laws in California might not be the same as in Nebraska. While all states have to follow the laws of the United States Constitution, some laws are unique to the state.

Draw a picture to illustrate the federal system of government.

There's a Theme

Organize the titles of books under the best theme.

The Story of Our Family

Summer in the Sun

The Happy Days of Summer

How to Make People Laugh

Diwali: Festival of Lights

Fun Activities to Do with Friends

Holidays	Making friends
Summer vacation	**Families**

Family Fun

Winter Celebrations

A Family in Need

MY BEST FRIEND JERRY

What I Did on Vacation

Christmas Around the World

Making the Most of It

Multiply.

1. $3.00
    $\times$ 4

2. $6.20
    $\times$ 5

3. $11.15
    $\times$ 7

4. $13.87
    $\times$ 9

5. $20.01 $\times$ 8 = _____

6. $91.76 $\times$ 3 = _____

7. $34.08 $\times$ 2 = _____

8. $75.33 $\times$ 6 = _____

Solve.

9. Carol washed the car and earned $4.25 every Saturday for four Saturdays. How much money did she earn? _____

10. Ruben sold 10 baseball cards for $.75 each. How much did he make?

_____

11. Olga knit 9 caps to sell for $8.45 each. What did she earn? _____

12. To make a kite, it costs the hobby shop $4.83 in materials. If they sell 8 kites for $9.83 each, what is their profit? _____

See and Be Seen

Read about each part of the eye. Then label each part on the diagram below.

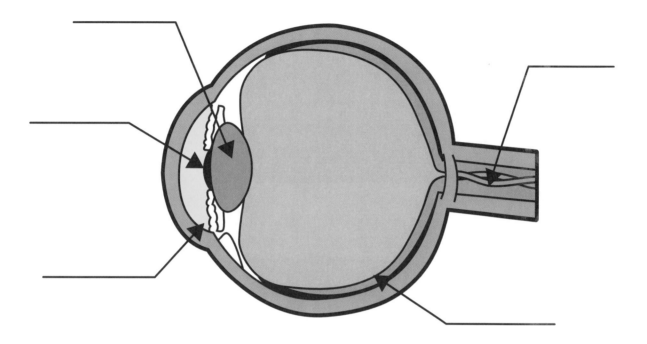

Cornea

This transparent layer protects the eye and allows light to enter the eyeball.

Pupil

This dark opening in the center of the colored iris controls how much light enters the eye.

Lens

Located behind the iris, the lens focuses light rays onto the retina.

Retina

The retina is a membrane lining the back of the eye. It contains special cells that react to light by sending signals to the brain through the optic nerve.

Optic Nerve

The optic nerve takes signals sent from the retina as electrical signals and delivers them to the brain. The brain then translates the signals into an image.

Plot the Story

Every story or movie has a plot. The plot is the skeleton of the story.
Fill in the chart using information about your favorite story or movie.

TITLE OF STORY OR MOVIE	
PROBLEM	
ACTION	
SOLUTION	
ENDING	

Dividing the Dough

Divide.

1. $15.00 ÷ 3 = _____

2. $40.00 ÷ 8 = _____

3. $48.00 ÷ 6 = _____

4. $357.28 ÷ 4 = _____

5. $462.00 ÷ 7 = _____

6. $56.97 ÷ 9 = _____

7. $34.02 ÷ 3 = _____

8. $67.00 ÷ 5 = _____

Solve.

9. Myra has $45.00 to buy soccer balls for the team. She can buy 9 of them with her budget. How much does each ball cost? _____

10. Mr. Tran gave his 3 children the same allowance. He gave a total of $27.00. How much did each child each get? _____

11. Ned collected $100.00 for charity from 10 businesses. If they each gave the same amount, how much did each business give? _____

12. Vivian paid $72.58 for 2 gifts. She paid the same item for both gifts. How much did she spend on each? What would her change be if she gave the clerk $75.00? _____

Poor Richard

Poor Richard's Almanac was published by Benjamin Franklin every year from 1733 to 1758. An almanac is a book that provides useful information such as weather predictions and practical solutions to household problems. Poor Richard's Almanac became most famous for its witty, influential sayings. Some of the most famous sayings include:

"A penny saved is a penny earned."

"Early to bed and early to rise, makes a man healthy, wealthy, and wise."

Think about values that are important to you. Write two short sayings that reflect your values. Draw a picture that illustrates your saying.

_____

_____

See the Scene

Identify the setting in each scene.

1. Martina and her family decided to go out for dinner. It was Friday night and they were hungry. Dad ordered pizza. Mom decided on pasta. Martina couldn't wait for the spumoni ice cream.

_____

2. The concrete was burning through my shoes. The air was so still it felt like I was inside an oven. The sun was burning into the top of my head. All the players were sweaty and hot. The basketball felt warm in my hands when Tyler passed it to me.

_____

3. Jackie and Bianca sat huddled together giggling. They had ice cream dripping down their arms as they licked their cones quickly. It was a fun afternoon sitting in the sunshine on the docks with their feet dangling in the water. The boat rocked gently against the dock and the girls laughed again.

_____

4. Jenna walked through the doors and couldn't believe her eyes. There were books stacked on shelves all the way to the ceiling. On the heavy wooden shelves, thousands and thousands of stories just waited to be explored.

_____

93

It's in the Bag

Read the clue. Choose the best answer and fill in the circle next to it.

1. The Walker family has 3 backpacks. One is for Amber, one is for Erica, and one is for Doug.

   ○ 3 × 3 = 9 backpacks
   ○ 1 + 1 + 1 = 3 backpacks
   ○ 3 × 3 × 3 = 27 backpacks

2. Kyle likes to take a few pictures on the hike. He takes 2 shots at every stop. They stop 5 times.

   ○ 2 + 5 = 7 shots
   ○ 2 × 5 = 10 shots
   ○ 2 × 10 = 20 shots

3. Doug makes sure that every hiker carries 2 bottles of water. Three people are hiking. How many bottles will they carry?

   ○ 2 × 3 = 6 bottles
   ○ 2 + 3 = 5 bottles
   ○ 2 × 6 = 12 bottles

4. Five members of the Runyon family joined Doug, Amber, and Erica on the hike.

   ○ 3 + 5 = 8 hikers
   ○ 3 × 5 = 15 hikers
   ○ 3 × 3 × 5 = 45 hikers

Read the clue and write an equation or expression.

5. Of the 8 people on the hike, 5 were children and 3 were adults.

   _____

6. Each of the 5 children ate 2 cookies. Ten cookies were enjoyed by the children.

   _____

A Bright Bulb

Use the diagram to answer the questions.

1. Look at the diagram. Based on the picture, write a brief description of how a series circuit works. _____

_____

_____

2. In a series circuit, what happens to the flow of electricity if one bulb is not working? Why does that happen? _____

_____

_____

3. Imagine there is a series circuit connected to an energy source. On the circuit is one light bulb. What do you think will happen to the brightness of that bulb if two more bulbs are added to the circuit? Why? _____

_____

_____

The Dancer

Tamika loved to dance. She started dancing when she was two years old. Her mother took her to ballet class. When the music started, Tamika began to spin. She felt so happy every time she slipped on her ballet shoes.

When Tamika was five she started taking tap dancing lessons. She told her mother she wanted to be a Broadway star and needed to learn to tap. "When I grow up, I'm going to be on stage," Tamika said to her mom.

Tamika grew into a tall, strong young woman. She took dance class every day. She took ballet, tap, hip-hop, jazz, modern, and even belly dancing. She wanted to learn every kind of dancing. She knew that she would need to know how to do all kinds of dancing to become a big star.

Answer the questions about the story.

1. Who is the main character? _____

2. What does the character do? _____

3. What does the character say? _____

_____

4. What kind of person would you say she is? What words or phrases tell you what kind of person she is? _____

_____

Movie Magic

Find the solution using the given information.

1. A movie ticket costs $8.00. If Spencer and Van have a twenty dollar bill, will they be able to see the movie?

_____ + _____ = _____ < _____

2. The theater manager has 2 deliveries of popcorn per week. Each delivery contains 53 pounds of popcorn. How many pounds of popcorn does she receive each week?

_____ × _____ = _____

3. Four hundred fans were seated in the theater for the special showing. Five sections divided them equally. How many fans were seated in Section C?

_____ ÷ _____ = _____

4. Thirty-five students were taking a trip to the movies. Small buses can hold 25 people. If there are 6 adult chaperones, how many buses are necessary?

_____ + _____ = _____ ÷ 25 = _____

5. Six friends decide to have a movie party. They each invite 2 guests. Each guest contributes $5.00. How much money is collected? Write your equation.

_____

Thomas Jefferson

Write a paragraph about Thomas Jefferson using the facts on this page.

Third president of the United States

Wrote the Declaration of Independence

Born in Virginia

Lived at Monticello, an estate in Virginia

Studied with tutors instead of going to formal schools

Helped found the United States Military Academy at West Point

Doubled the size of the nation with the Louisiana Purchase

Elected president in 1800

Asked Meriwether Lewis to lead an exploration of the new land in the Northwest Territory

Helped create the University of Virginia

_____

_____

_____

_____

_____

_____

_____

_____

Form a Fable

A fable is a story that gives animals or objects human qualities. Fables usually have a moral or message.

One famous example of a fable is the story of the tortoise and the hare. In that well-known tale, a timid tortoise finally gets tired of hearing a boastful hare brag about how fast he can run. The tortoise challenges the hare to a race. Because the hare believes his natural speed will make him the winner, he doesn't give the race his best effort. In fact, he takes a break and falls asleep under a tree. While the hare naps, the tortoise creeps across the finish line and wins the race. "Slow and steady wins the race" is a famous saying that comes from the moral of this fable.

Write your own fable. Remember to include animals with human qualities.
Also be sure to give your fable a moral.

_____

_____

_____

_____

_____

_____

_____

_____

_____

_____

Sporty Signs

Insert the correct mathematical symbol to make the statement true.

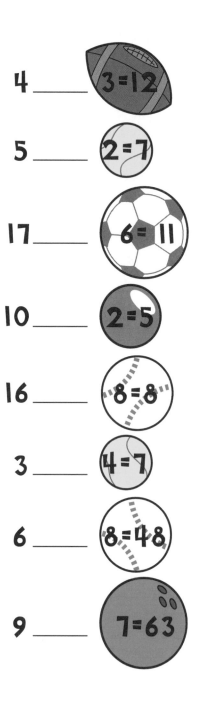

4 _____ 3 = 12

5 _____ 2 = 7

17 _____ 6 = 11

10 _____ 2 = 5

16 _____ 8 = 8

3 _____ 4 = 7

6 _____ 8 = 48

9 _____ 7 = 63

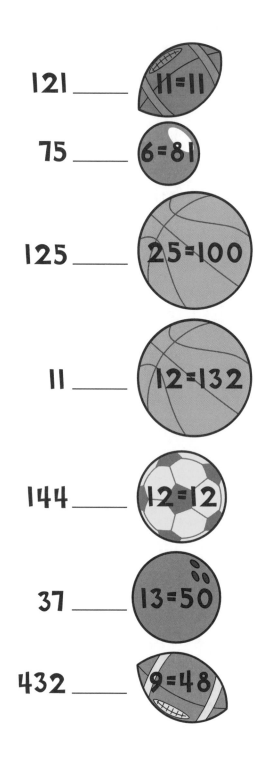

121 _____ 11 = 11

75 _____ 6 = 81

125 _____ 25 = 100

11 _____ 12 = 132

144 _____ 12 = 12

37 _____ 13 = 50

432 _____ 9 = 48

Pointing North

Ask an adult to help you as you follow these steps to build a simple compass.

Step 1: Gather the followings supplies:

    clear glass or plastic container

    magnet

    needle

    small piece of cork

Step 2: Rub the magnet in one direction along the length of the needle about 30 or 40 times.

Step 3: Put the needle through the cork.

Step 4: Fill the container with water.

Step 5: Carefully place the piece of cork with the needle into the container. The cork should float on the surface of the water.

Step 6: Place the container on a table. Watch as the needle settles. The thickest part of the needle will point north.

Step 7: Take your compass to different locations indoors and outdoors.

Write a paragraph describing the results of your observations.

_____

_____

_____

_____

_____

Make a Legend

A legend is a story based on a real person or event. One example is a famous story about George Washington. According to the legend, when George was a child, he received a little axe as a gift. He went excitedly to his garden and started cutting down plants. He came to his father's cherry tree and, taking a swing, accidentally cut it down. When George's father saw what happened, he was very angry and asked, "Who cut down my favorite tree?"

George said, "I cannot tell a lie, Father. It was I, with my little hatchet."

While no one knows if this story is actually true, it has been passed down through history, probably because it shows that George Washington was a very honest person. Legends often tell tales of bravery and strength.

Write your own legend about a historical event or person. Use facts to create a story.

_____

_____

_____

_____

_____

_____

_____

_____

_____

_____

Give an Inch

Use the information in the chart to solve the problems below. Convert each measurement.

1. 12 inches = _____ foot

2. 36 inches = _____ feet

3. 72 inches = _____ feet

4. 108 inches = _____ feet

5. 144 inches = _____ feet

6. 3 feet = _____ yard

7. 6 feet = _____ yards

8. 66 feet = _____ yards

9. 108 feet = _____ yards

10. 366 feet = _____ yards

11. 5,280 feet = _____ mile

12. 15,840 feet = _____ miles

13. 52,800 feet = _____ miles

14. 126,720 feet = _____ miles

15. 264,000 feet = _____ miles

Conversions	
12 inches	1 Foot
3 Feet	1 yard
5,280 feet	1 mile

Douglass Speaks Out

Use the words in the word bank to complete the crossword puzzle about Frederick Douglass.

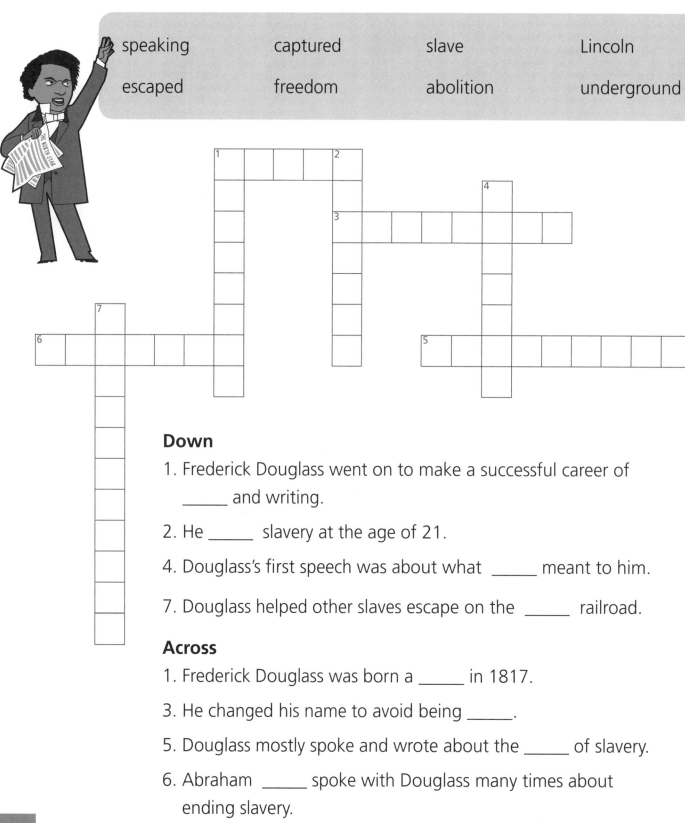

speaking   captured   slave   Lincoln

escaped   freedom   abolition   underground

Down

1. Frederick Douglass went on to make a successful career of _____ and writing.

2. He _____ slavery at the age of 21.

4. Douglass's first speech was about what _____ meant to him.

7. Douglass helped other slaves escape on the _____ railroad.

Across

1. Frederick Douglass was born a _____ in 1817.

3. He changed his name to avoid being _____.

5. Douglass mostly spoke and wrote about the _____ of slavery.

6. Abraham _____ spoke with Douglass many times about ending slavery.

What Kind of Character

Characters are very important to stories. When you write a story, how do you decide what your characters are like? Look at the following characters and write a description for each.

1. a ten-year old boy

wears a worn out baseball cap

_____

_____

_____

2. a grandmother

enjoys planting roses in her garden

_____

_____

_____

3. a three-year old girl

draws with a purple crayon

_____

_____

_____

4. a teacher

works at her computer

_____

_____

_____

Summer Reading

Use the Commutative Property to complete each set.

If 3 × 4 = 12   If 2 × 8 = __
then 4 × __ = 12   then 8 × __ = __

If 3 × 2 = __   If 5 × 9 = __
then 2 × __ = __   then 9 × __ = __

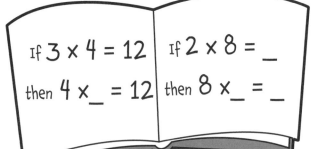

If 4 × 2 = __   If 1 × 9 = __
then 2 × 4 = __   then __ × 1 = __

If 3 × 7 = __   If 2 × 6 = __
then __ × 3 = __   then __ × 2 = __

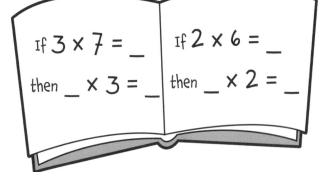

If 4 × 9 = __   If 5 × 3 = __
then 9 × __ = __   then 3 × __ = __

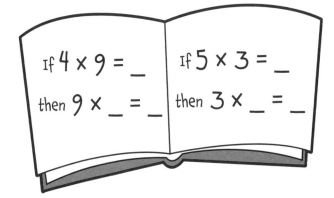

Dig In!

Kaley, Judah, Brooke, Asher, Ali, and Delia each ordered a different dinner. They ordered a steak, a hamburger, a slice of pizza, chicken nuggets, cobb salad, and lasagna. Use the clues to match each child with his or her dinner.

- Brooke's dinner came on a bun with fries.
- The name of Judah's dinner begins with a "C."
- Delia doesn't eat red meat.
- Kaley's dinner is served cold.
- Ali's dinner came with three different toppings.

	Steak	Hamburger	Pizza	Chicken	Cobb Salad	Lasagna
Kaley						
Judah						
Brooke						
Asher						
Ali						
Delia						

Yard Sale

Use the advertisement to answer the questions.

Giant Yard Sale

Saturday, June 30th

8am to 3pm   Four Families on Cypress Grove Road

toys, furniture, appliances, clothing, trading cards

➡ Great Deals! ⬅

1. On what day is the yard sale going to happen? _____

2. What time will the sale be going on? _____

3. How many families will participate in the sale? _____

4. Where will the sale happen? _____

5. If you wanted to buy trading cards would you go to the sale? _____

6. If you wanted to buy a car, do you think this might be a good place to look for one? _____

A Perfect Pair

Use the Associative Property to complete each set.

1. If $2 \times 4 \times 3 = 24$, then $3 \times 4 \times 2 =$ _____.

2. If $6 \times 1 \times 2 = 12$, then $2 \times 1 \times 6 =$ _____.

3. If $9 \times 2 \times 3 = 54$, then $3 \times 2 \times$ _____ $= 54$.

4. If $2 \times 2 \times 6 = 24$, then $2 \times$ _____ $\times 2 = 24$.

5. If $5 \times 3 \times 7 = 105$, then $7 \times 3 \times 5 =$ _____.

6. If $3 \times 9 \times 4 =$ _____, then $9 \times$ _____ $\times 4 = 108$.

7. If $2 \times 3 \times 8 = 48$, then $3 \times 2 \times 8 =$ _____.

8. If $9 \times 1 \times 7 = 63$, then $7 \times 1 \times$ _____ $= 63$.

9. If $4 \times 5 \times 3 = 60$, then _____ $\times 5 \times 4 = 60$.

10. If $8 \times 7 \times 4 = 224$, then $4 \times 7 \times 8 =$ _____.

Draw a picture using objects to illustrate the Associative Property.

No More Grapes

Cesar Chavez organized farm workers to form unions. The unions gave the workers strength in numbers. They gained better pay and better working conditions. Mr. Chavez worked hard to get the farm owners to work with the labor unions. When the owners wouldn't, Chavez led a widespread boycott of all grapes and lettuce grown in California. That meant that people were encouraged to not buy grapes or lettuce until the owners accepted the unions. Eventually, the owners agreed to work with the unions and workers' rights were improved.

Design a poster advertising the grape and lettuce boycott. Do some research about Cesar Chavez and farm unions, if necessary. What should people know about the boycott?

Smile for Similes

Similes are comparisons that use *like* or *as*. Metaphors are comparisons that do not use *like* or *as*.

simile: Olivia ran like a gazelle across the field.

metaphor: Olivia is a gazelle when she runs across the field.

Write a simile or metaphor for each picture.

1. _____

_____

2. _____

_____

3. _____

_____

4. _____

_____

5. _____

_____

6. _____

_____

Think It Through

Alfonso and Gilbert worked to solve the same problem. They each chose their own way and still got the same result. Explain why both ways worked.

Alfonso	**Gilbert**

Alfonso

$$892$$
$$\times\ \ 36$$
$$5,352$$
$$+\ 26,760$$
$$32,112$$

Gilbert

$$892$$
$$\times\ \ 6$$
$$5,352$$

$$892$$
$$\times\ \ 30$$
$$26,760$$

$$5,352$$
$$+\ 26,760$$
$$32,112$$

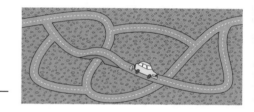

_____

_____

_____

Solve each problem in two ways.

1. $482 \times 26 =$

_____

_____

2. $5,150 \times 29 =$

_____

_____

3. $5,844 \times 16 =$

_____

_____

Life Under the Sea

A coral reef is a type of underwater environment made from the skeletons of marine animals called corals. Each reef is an ecosystem, or community of living things. Crabs, clams, lobsters, sea anemones, sea stars, and sponges are just some of the invertebrates that make the reefs their homes. Stunning arrays of colorful fish also live in these reefs. Many have special adaptations, or characteristics that allow them to survive in the coral reef environment. For example, parrotfish use their beaklike front teeth to scrape food from the hard corals. The moray eel's thin body makes it easy to swim through narrow cracks in the reef where it can hide and wait for prey.

Many of these reef creatures benefit from symbiotic relationships. In symbiosis, two different organisms live together in a way that helps one or more of them. For instance, small fish called wrasses feed on parasites from the bodies of larger fish. The smaller fish get food and the bigger fish stay clean!

Answer the questions about the reading.

1. What is an ecosystem? _____

_____

2. What is an adaptation? _____

_____

3. Give an example of an adaptation in an animal that lives on or near a coral reef.

_____

4. What is a symbiotic relationship? _____

_____

5. Give an example of a symbiotic relationship between two animals that live on or near a coral reef. _____

_____

A Personification Situation

Personification is when animals or other inanimate objects are given human qualities. Write a script for an exchange between the two animals or objects described below.

1. a lazy pig and a giggling goose

_____

_____

_____

_____

2. an old window and the curious cat

_____

_____

_____

_____

3. a smelly shoe and a sock with holes in the toe

_____

_____

_____

_____

I'll Take a Dozen!

Each price shown above is for one item. Solve to find the
total cost of each bakery order. Show your work.

1. A dozen donuts to celebrate a big win

2. 18 cream puffs for a tea party

3. 9 cupcakes for Nina's ninth birthday

4. 2 pies for a special guest

5. 6 muffins for a brunch

6. 3 cookies for your friends

Mr. President

Read the paragraph about nine important events in the life of President Barack Obama. Insert the dates and descriptions onto the timeline.

In 1961, Barack Obama was born in Honolulu, Hawaii to parents Ann Dunham and Barack Obama, Sr. Six years later, he moved to Indonesia with his mother and stepfather. In 1971, he returned to Hawaii to attend Punahou School in Honolulu. He graduated from Columbia University in 1983. Eight years later, he graduated from Harvard Law School. The next year, he married Michelle Robinson. Obama was elected to the Illinois Senate in 1996. Eight years later, he was elected to the United States Senate in an overwhelming win over Alan Keyes. In 2008, Obama was elected the President of the United States.

1961: Barack Obama is born

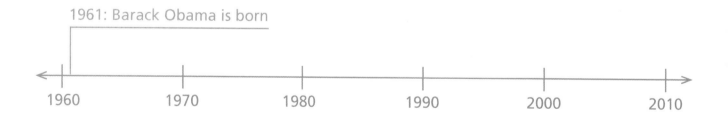

1960 1970 1980 1990 2000 2010

Write a Sandwich

When you write an essay or report, every paragraph should have a topic sentence and supporting details. Use the frame below to draft a paragraph about foods you eat at lunch.

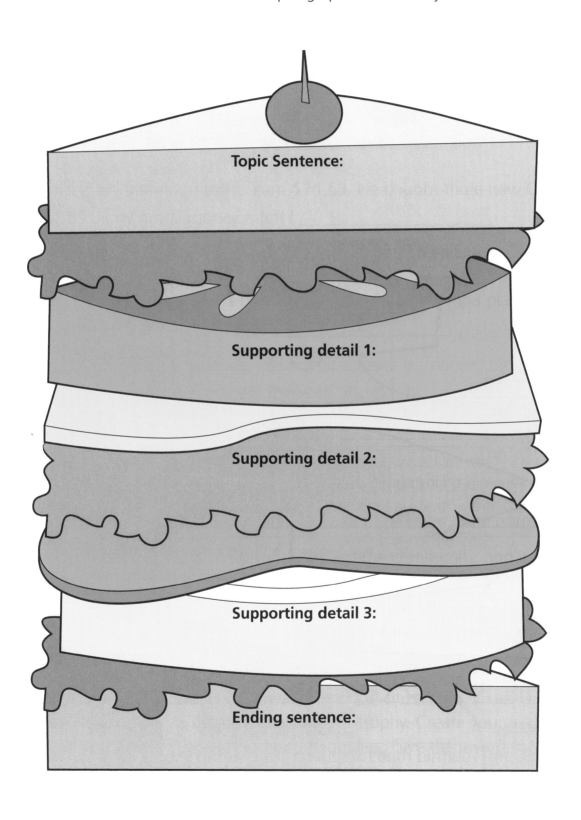

Topic Sentence:

Supporting detail 1:

Supporting detail 2:

Supporting detail 3:

Ending sentence:

Two by Two

Write a number sentence and solve each problem.

1. Four people stood on the stage. How many feet were on the stage?

_____

2. Spiders have 8 legs. If you were going to make sneakers for 8 spiders, how many tiny shoes do you need to make?

_____

3. Mrs. Leahey's science class did an experiment. It required 3 test tubes per group. How many test tubes were needed for 5 groups?

_____

4. Deshon washes cars to earn spending money. It takes 3 minutes to wash a tire. How long does he spend washing the tires on one car?

_____

5. The Cole family went on vacation for 9 days. They had 2 messages left on their phone each day. How many messages were waiting for them when they returned?

_____

Life in the Desert

 Cactus plants have many adaptations that allow them to survive in the hot, dry desert environments where they grow. Their thick, fleshy stems hold water, allowing the plants to thrive between rain showers. Their waxy skin keeps water from evaporating. Cacti also have very long, thick roots to help them store water beneath the ground and to gather nutrients from the earth. The desert plants grow far apart from one another so they do not need to compete for the scarce resources the environment offers. To protect themselves from hungry desert animals, cacti have prickly spines. In addition to scaring off predators, these spines provide some shade from the blazing sun.

Answer the questions about the reading.

1. What are two adaptations that allow the cactus to store water?

_____

_____

2. What is an adaptation that protects the cactus from predators?

_____

3. Do you think human beings have adaptations that make them suited for life in the desert? Why or why not? _____

_____

4. Using the Internet or an encyclopedia, research a desert animal, such as a camel, a rattlesnake, or a jackrabbit. On a separate piece of paper, write a short paragraph that tells about the characteristics of the animal that allow it to survive in a hot, dry desert environment.

Prepare to Write

Later in this book, you will be asked to write an essay about an important event in your life. To prepare, brainstorm about the event. In the center of the graphic organizer below, write the name of your special event. Fill the outer circles of the organizer with details about it, such as the time and place, the names of the people who were included, and describing words that tell about the day.

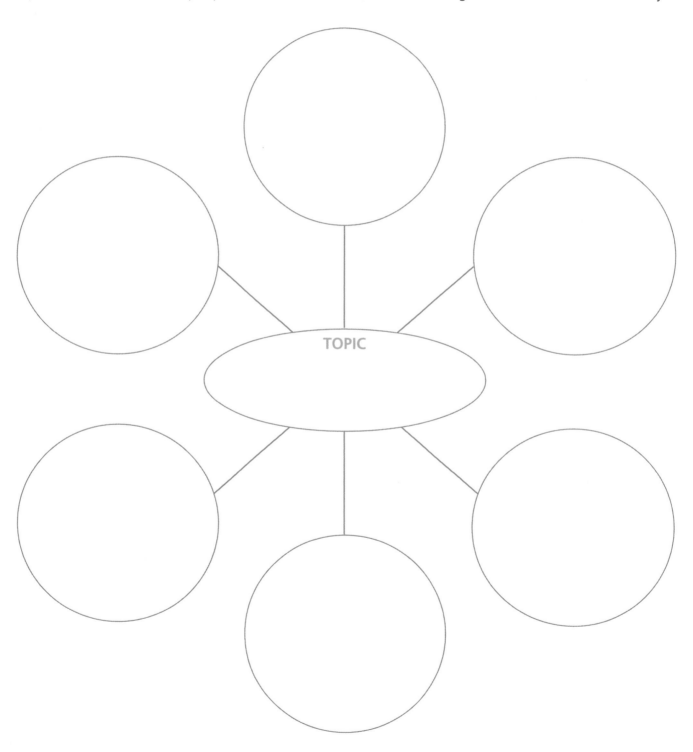

TOPIC

Proper Equipment

Tool:	Task:	Customary Units:	Metric Units:
measuring cup with fl oz	measure liquid volume	fl oz/ cup/ pt	mL/L
ruler	measure length	in/ft	mm/cm/m
scale	measure weight/ mass	oz/lb	mg/g/kg

Study the chart to answer the questions.

1. To measure the weight of an adult man, what tool will you need? _____

2. To determine the volume of a pitcher of tea, what tool would you use? _____

3. To find the height of a door, what tool would be helpful? _____

Tell what is being measured: volume, length, or weight/mass.

4. a 90 inch couch _____

5. a 180 pound gorilla _____

6. two cups of milk _____

Measure. Use customary or metric units.

7. your weight _____

8. a glass of chocolate milk _____

9. the width of a door _____

Cool Consumers

Define each term. Provide an example for each.

Producer

Definition _____

_____

Example_____

_____

Consumer

Definition _____

_____

Example_____

_____

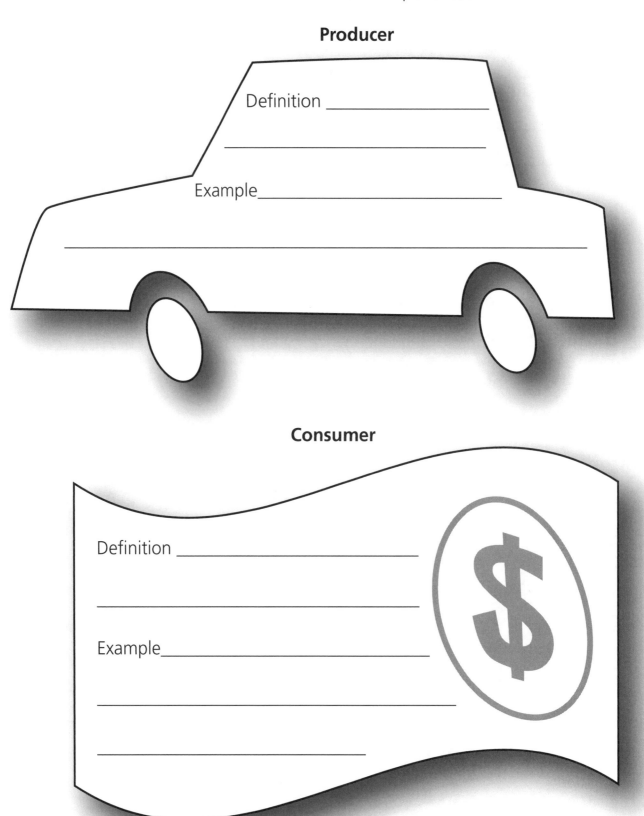

Writing a Draft

The second step in the writing process is writing a draft. Look back at what you did during prewriting on page 120. Notice how your ideas are organized. If you have several ideas grouped together, these will form a paragraph. Write out each paragraph with the ideas you brainstormed earlier.

_____

_____

_____

_____

_____

_____

_____

_____

_____

_____

_____

_____

_____

_____

_____

Get Results!

Circle the correct tool for measuring.

1. Weight of a watermelon: ruler   scale   measuring cup

2. Height of a fence: scale   meter stick   measuring cup

3. Volume of a milk carton: measuring cup   tape measure   scale

4. Length of a book: scale   ruler   tape measure

5. Distance across a field: tape measure   scale   ruler

6. Mass of a baseball: scale   tape measure   measuring cup

7. Volume of a sink: meter stick   measuring cup   scale

8. Weight of a cat: scale   tape measure   measuring cup

9. Volume of a water balloon: meter stick   ruler   measuring cup

10. Distance a car has traveled: speedometer   odometer   pedometer

ON YOUR OWN	Choose three items described above. Measure them using metric units.

124

A Bearable Life

North of the Arctic Circle, the land has a cover of ice and snow for most of the year. The cold, dry, treeless regions in this part of the world are known as tundra. These areas have constant daylight in midsummer and never-ending darkness in midwinter. Tundra regions experience bitter winters. Even the warmest summer days reach only about 50°F (10°C). Plant-eating animals feed on the plants that thrive in the permanently frozen soil, while carnivores eat smaller animals to survive.

Write a story about life on the tundra from the perspective of a polar bear.
Do some research to help you.

Read and Revise

The third step in the writing process is to revise your work. Look back at the paragraphs you wrote on page 123. Read them over carefully. Ask yourself the following questions.

What can I change to make it sound more interesting?

Where do I need to add more details?

Are all of my facts correct?

Do all of my paragraphs have a beginning, middle, and end?

Make any corrections. Rewrite your paragraph below.

_____

_____

_____

_____

_____

_____

_____

_____

_____

_____

_____

Find the Volume

To determine the volume of a solid, multiply the length, width, and height.

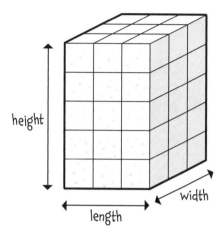

height

width

length

Give the volume of the solids.

1.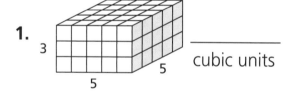
3
5
5
_____ cubic units

2.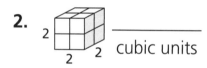
2
2   2
_____ cubic units

3.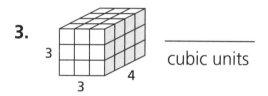
3
3   4
_____ cubic units

4.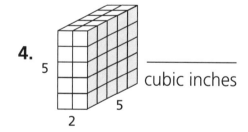
5
5
2
_____ cubic inches

5.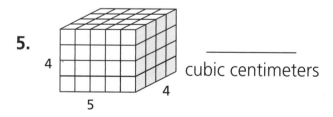
4
5   4
_____ cubic centimeters

6.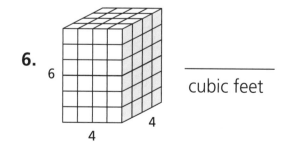
6
4   4
_____ cubic feet

Going for Goods

Think about an object you use every day, such as a microwave or television.
Find out where the device was made. Then answer the questions.

1. How do you think the object arrived in the United States? _____

_____

2. Why do you think this object was imported to the United States? _____

_____

3. What are the advantages to buying a product made in a foreign country? _____

_____

4. What are the advantages of buying a product made locally? _____

_____

5. Name three products manufactured in your city or state. Use the Internet to help
you find this information, if necessary. _____

_____

6. Do you think it's important to buy products made in the United States? Why or
why not? _____

_____

Edit for Elegance

The fourth step in the writing process is editing. Read the revised essay you wrote on page 126. At this point you will correct any mistakes. Look for the following:

punctuation errors

spelling errors

grammatical errors

missing words or letters

Rewrite your essay below. Make all necessary corrections in spelling, grammar, and punctuation.

_____

_____

_____

_____

_____

_____

_____

_____

_____

_____

_____

It's No Small Matter

Circle the most appropriate measurement and tell what is being measured: mass, volume, or length.

1. soda   355 mL   355 L   355 kL   _____

2. potato   560 g   560 mg   560 kg   _____

3. sailboat   12 m   12 km   12mm   _____

4. soccer field 91 km   91 cm   91 m   _____

5. car   1,200 kg   1,200 mg   1,200 g   _____

6. couch   2 cm   2 m   2 km   _____

7. bucket   10 L   10 mL   10 kL   _____

8. gas tank 57 kL   57 L   57 mL   _____

9. bicycle   1 cm   1 mm   1 m   _____

10. pie   1 mg   1 kg   1 g   _____

Full Forests

Read the paragraphs, then compare and contrast rainforests with temperate deciduous forests by completing the Venn diagram.

Temperate deciduous forests grow in regions that experience warm summers and cold winters. The canopy, or tallest layer of branches and leaves, is about 100 feet high in a temperate forest. There are about 15 to 25 different kinds of trees. Most of them shed their leaves in fall. The forests are home to birds, insects, and large mammals like bears and deer. Small mammals such as mice, skunks, opossums, and squirrels also live here. During the cold winter months, some of the mammals hibernate. Many of the birds migrate south to warmer climates.

Tropical rain forests grow in regions near the equator where the climate is warm all year long. As many as 100 different kinds of trees grow in these forests, where the canopies can reach 165 feet. Nearly all the trees of tropical rain forests are broadleaf evergreens, meaning they stay green throughout the year. The rainforests are the year-round home to bats, birds, insects, lizards, mice, monkeys, opossums, sloths, and snakes. In fact, there are more species of mammals, fish, insects, and birds in tropical rainforests than in any other place on earth!

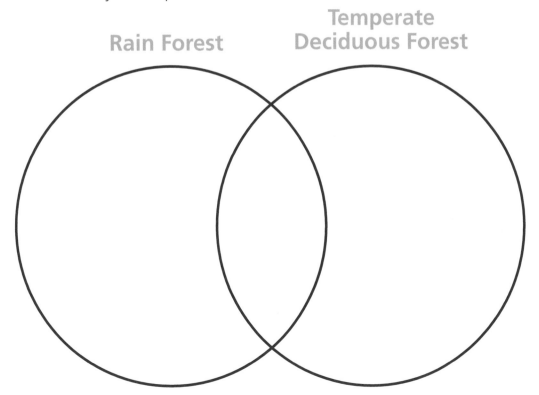

Rain Forest

Temperate Deciduous Forest

Published Prose

Once you finish a piece of writing, it's time to publish your work! You can do this in lots of different ways. You can read it to friends and family, send your work to a local newspaper, or create a digital video presentation. Another option is to create a book with illustrations. In the space below, create a cover for the essay you wrote on page 129. Be sure to include the title of the essay and the name of the author—you!

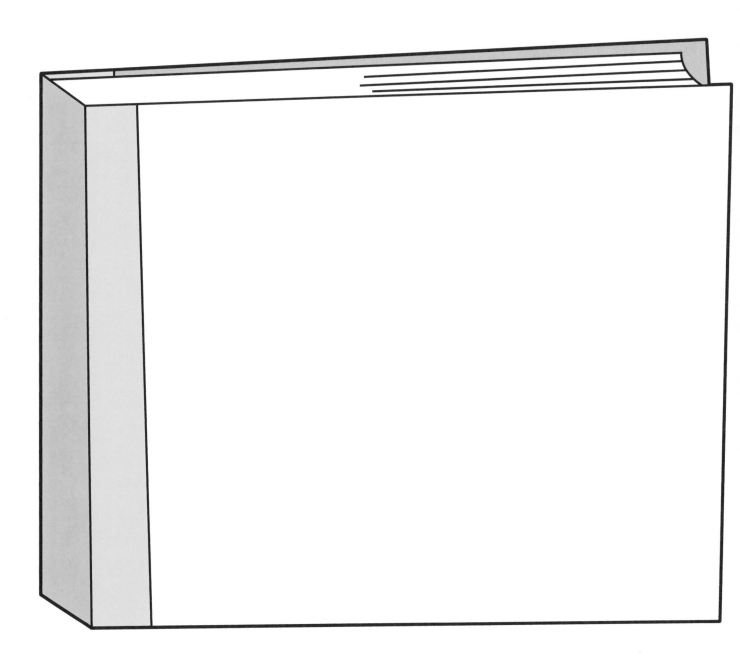

Here to There

Supply the unit of customary measurement: ounce, pound, inch, gallon, or yard.

1. Length of a pen   6 _____

2. Volume of liquid soap   10 _____

3. Weight of a bunch of bananas   20 _____

4. Height of a 10 year old   58 _____

5. Volume of a car's gas tank   15 _____

6. Weight of a dictionary $\frac{1}{2}$ _____

7. Length of an adult foot   12 _____

8. Mass of a pumpkin   5 _____

9. Weight of a dolphin   400 _____

10. Length of a football field   100 _____

Measure the following items and record your results with the appropriate customary unit below.

11. height of a door frame   _____

12. diameter of a dinner plate   _____

13. weight of a loaf of bread   _____

14. volume of one juice box   _____

15. weight of one apple   _____

Build a Budget

Jaden makes $35 a month mowing lawns in his neighborhood. He also receives $20 a month in allowance. He usually spends $5 a week on snacks and $10 a month on comic books. The rest he saves.

Make a monthly budget for Jaden using what you know.

Money earned	
Money spent	
Money saved	

1. Jaden wants to buy a video game system that costs $300. How many months will it take him to save enough to buy the system? _____

2. If Jaden stops spending money on comic books and snacks, how many months will it take him to save enough for his game system? _____

Makes Sense

Sensory details add descriptive information about how things feel, sound, smell, taste, or look. Use sensory details to expand each sentence into a descriptive paragraph.

The picnic was fun. _____

_____

_____

_____

_____

Melissa watched the fireworks. _____

_____

_____

_____

_____

The leaves on the tree are green. _____

_____

_____

_____

_____

Brick by Brick

To determine the **area** of a rectangle or square, multiply the length times the width.

width

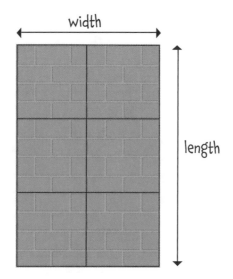

length

Give the area of the shapes.

1. _____ square units

2. _____ square units

3. 3 inches, 5 inches _____ square inches

4. 10 cm, 6 cm _____ square centimeters

5. _____ square units

6. 3 feet, 12 feet _____ square feet

Playing in the Grass

Read the paragraph below. Then write a story that uses at least two prairie animals as characters. Be sure to include details about the prairie environment in your story.

North American prairies are grasslands that cover most of Texas, Oklahoma, Kansas, Nebraska, Iowa, Illinois, South Dakota, and North Dakota. The many different kinds of grasses that grow in these areas can reach heights of six feet! Asters, blazing stars, coneflowers, goldenrods, and sunflowers are just some of the colorful wildflowers that dot the prairies. Cottonwood, oak, and willow trees thrive there, too. Animals such as rabbits, mice, prairie dogs, and deer feed on these prairie plants. Meadowlarks, quail, and sparrows build their nests in the prairies' thick cover. Coyotes, foxes, and skunks eat both plants and smaller prairie animals. Insects like grasshoppers and leafhoppers are also common on the prairie.

_____

_____

_____

_____

_____

_____

_____

_____

Camp Query

Imagine you are researching summer camps. Write a formal letter to request information from a camp you want to attend. Make sure to include the following:

address   return address   date   salutation   body of letter   closing   signature

ON YOUR OWN

Create your own brochure for a summer camp. What kind of camp would you run? Use your computer or paper and markers to create an advertising brochure.

'Round the Outside

Name the polygon and find the perimeter using a centimeter ruler.

1.

Polygon _____

Perimeter _____

2.

Polygon _____

Perimeter _____

3. Polygon _____

Perimeter _____

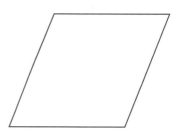

4.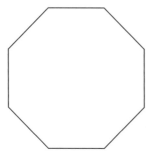

Polygon _____

Perimeter _____

5.

Polygon _____

Perimeter _____

6.

Polygon _____

Perimeter _____

Endangered Everglades

The Everglades is a wetlands area in Florida. Over the last century, much of it has been damaged or destroyed by humans. Today the Everglades National Park covers about 1,500,000 acres, but the park is only about one-fifth of the size of the Everglades' original area. In the early 1900s, the state began to drain water from the area to make farmland. Later, water from the area was used to supply drinking water to growing communities in southern Florida. In the 1940s, the government designated the southwestern region of the area a national park. But the area continued to be damaged by the growth of cities and the agricultural industry, which demanded large supplies of water. In addition, chemicals from area farms leaked into the area water supply. Both plants and animals suffered as a result.

Answer the questions about the reading.

1. Name three factors that have contributed to the destruction of the Everglades.

_____

_____

2. Name one thing that the government has done to preserve the Everglades.

_____

_____

3. Using the Internet or other resources, research plant and animal life in the Everglades. Then use that information, along with what you learned in the paragraph above, to write a persuasive essay on the importance of saving the Everglades on another piece of paper.

A Proper Thank You

Imagine your favorite author came to your school for a visit. Write a thank you letter to the author. Make sure to include the following:

date   salutation   body of letter   closing   signature

ON YOUR OWN

Find out which publishing company publishes your favorite author's books. See if there is a website on which you can email your favorite author. Write him or her a note telling why you enjoy the book so much.

Inch by Inch

Divide to convert smaller units to larger units.

Example:

> 32 oz = _____ lb
>
> 32 oz = 32 ÷ 16
>
> 32 oz = 2 lb

Multiply to convert larger units to smaller units.

Example:

> 6 km = _____ m
>
> 6 km = 6 x 1,000
>
> 6 km = 6,000 m

Convert these customary units.

1. 2 ft = _____ in

2. 13 lb = _____ oz

3. 60 in = _____ ft

4. 3 c = _____ oz

5. 20 oz = _____ lb _____ oz

> **Length: 12 in = 1 ft**
>
> **Weight: 16 oz = 1 lb**
>
> **Volume: 8 fl oz = 1 cup**

Convert these metric units.

6. 400 cm = _____ m

7. 5 kg = _____ g

8. 10 L = _____ mL

9. 1,000g = _____ kg

10. 25 m = _____ cm

> **Length: 1 m = 100 cm**
>
> **Weight: 1,000 oz = 1 kg**
>
> **Volume: 1,000 mL = 1 L**

Plenty of Planets

Using the Internet or an encyclopedia, do some research about the planets in our solar system. Fill in the chart below.

Planet	Average Distance from the Sun	Characteristics
Mercury		
Venus		
Earth		
Mars		
Jupiter		
Saturn		
Uranus		
Neptune		

ON YOUR OWN

Make a model of the solar system. Use foam, wire, and paint to represent the sun and planets. Show your creation to your friends and family and explain each object.

Sticky Sentences

Identify each sentence as declarative, interrogative, exclamatory, or imperative.

1. Ernie's ice cream cone dripped down his arm as he enjoyed the hot summer sun.

   _____

2. The sidewalk was as hot as lava under our feet._____

3. What kind of popsicle would you like?_____

4. Put on lots of sunscreen._____

5. What a hot day!_____

6. The sand sticks like glue to Gina's sweaty skin._____

7. Lonia spilled lemonade down the front of her favorite t-shirt._____

8. Strawberries leave bright red rings around my mouth when I eat them._____

9. Turn the crank on the ice cream maker._____

10. Will you turn on the hose so we can make mud pies?_____

11. Raymond's chocolate bar melted on the backseat of the hot car._____

12. Watch out! The bubble gum is going to get stuck in your hair!_____

Silly Sides

Find the area and perimeter of each shape.

Area	Perimeter

1. A = _____   P = _____

2. A = _____   P = _____

3. A = _____   P = _____

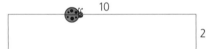

4. A = _____   P = _____

5. A = _____   P = _____

6. A = _____   P = _____

ON YOUR OWN	Draw two different rectangles that have the same area. Give the perimeter of each.

145

Stellar's Sea Cow

The extinct Stellar's sea cow belonged to the same scientific family as manatees and dugongs. Named by naturalist Georg Wilhelm Steller in 1741, Stellar's sea cows were aquatic herbivores. They had no teeth. They ate sea grasses, such as kelp, by tearing it with their mouths. They looked similar to whales and sea lions—and were actually related to elephants! These huge creatures were up to 28 feet long and weighed as much as 8 tons. A thick layer of fat protected the sea cow from the cold waters off the coast of Alaska and Russia where they lived in herds. Native Aleut and Eskimo people hunted them for their meat and fat. In the late 1700s, fur hunters flocked to the islands near the sea cows' habitats and, discovering that that the creatures made for a great source of food, hunted them to extinction in a period of less than 30 years.

In an acrostic poem, the first letter of each line is part of a word or name. Write an acrostic poem about the Stellar's sea cow. The first line has been written for you.

S wimmer_____

T _____

E _____

L _____

L _____

A _____   S _____   C _____

R _____   E _____   O _____

S _____   A _____   W _____

Ride the Agreement Train

Underline the subject in each sentence. Circle the verb. If the subject and verb don't agree, rewrite the sentence.

1. The train roars into the station.

_____

2. The conductor shout "All aboard!".

_____

3. Passengers scrambles to get on the train.

_____

4. Luggage are hauled into the storage compartment.

_____

5. Kenisha and Trent is very excited to pull out of the station.

_____

6. The giant engine rumbles as the wheels begin to turn.

_____

7. The sleek train speed along the track.

_____

8. Kenisha look out the window

_____

9. Trent takes a picture

_____

10. They feels happy to be on their first train ride.

_____

Amusing Areas

Complete the table.

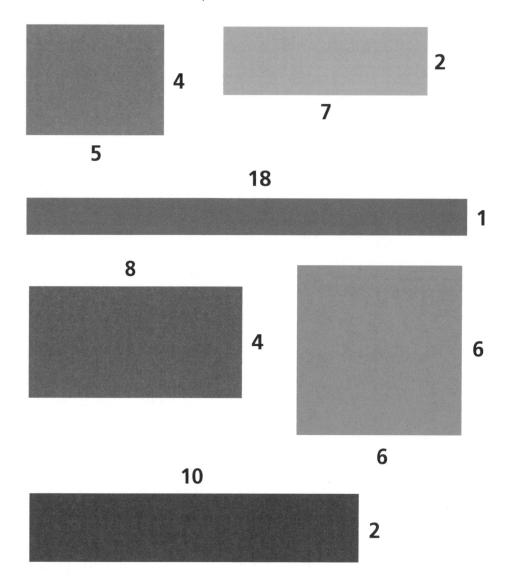

Arrangement	Perimeter	Area
1. 4 in. x 5 in.		
2. 2 cm x 7 cm		
3. 1 yd. x 18 yd.		
4. 4 ft. x 8 ft.		
5. 6 in. x 6 in.		
6. 2 mi. x 10 mi.		

Star Showers

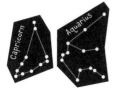

"Shooting stars" and "falling stars" are both names that people have used for many hundreds of years to describe meteors. These bright streaks of light across the night sky are actually caused by small bits of rock and debris, called meteoroids. Thirty to eighty miles above the ground and traveling at thousands of miles an hour, meteoroids quickly ignite in the friction of the atmosphere. As they crash and burn high in Earth's upper atmosphere, they seem to "shoot" across the sky. A meteoroid's intense brightness might make you think it is a star. Almost all meteoroids are destroyed before they reach Earth. The rare few that survive and hit the ground are known as meteorites. If you're lucky enough to spot a meteorite and see where it hits, it's easy to think you just saw a star "fall."

1. "Shooting stars" are actually

    a. stars falling from space.

    b. small bits of rock and debris burning high in the atmosphere.

    c. rockets.

2. What does the word *ignite* mean in this passage?

    a. catch fire

    b. travel quickly

    c. fall

3. Why do people confuse meteoroids for stars?

    a. They are intensely bright.

    b. They are made of rock.

    c. They land on Earth.

4. Meteorites are rare because

    a. they are made of debris.

    b. they are stars.

    c. few meteoroids survive the fall to Earth.

A Day at the Zoo

Choose the correct pronoun for each sentence or group of sentences.

1. Paola and Ben went to the zoo. _____ arrived at 10:00 in the morning.

   a. He   **b.** She   **c.** It   **d.** They

2. The giant python rested in dark cave. Will _____ emerge later today?

   a. they   **b.** it   **c.** us   **d.** we

3. Dozens of pink flamingoes fluffed _____ feathers at Paola and Ben.

   a. her   **b.** his   **c.** their   **d.** them

4. The zookeeper fed the monkeys at 12:30. _____ fed them bananas.

   a. She   **b.** They   **c.** We   **d.** It

5. Paola and Ben watched as the newborn fawn tried to stand. _____ legs wobbled.

   a. Their   **b.** Our   **c.** Its   **d.** Her

FAST FACT

Zoologists study animals in zoos and in the wild. They study how animals behave, how they eat, and how they live. Zoologists use their knowledge to help animals get better if they are sick and give them a comfortable environment in the zoo.

Divide and Solve

To find the area of a complex shape, divide it into basic shapes.

Example: 8 square inches + 4 square inches = 12 square inches

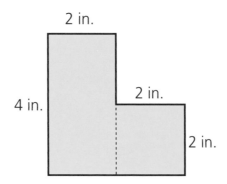

2 in.

4 in.

2 in.

2 in.

4 inches X 2 inches = 8 in.^{2}
2 inches X 2 inches = 4 in.^{2}
Area = 12 square inches

Use what you know about area to solve.

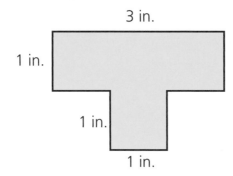

3 in.

1 in.

1 in.

1 in.

Using a dotted line, divide the space into one rectangle and one square.

1. What is the area of the rectangle? _____

What is the area of the square? _____

2. What is the total area of the shape? _____

3. Make a complex shape of your own and give the area and perimeter.

The Lunar Cycle

Draw a picture of each phase of the lunar cycle. Write a brief description of each stage.

New moon

First quarter

Full moon

Last quarter

Add Some Adjectives

Write two adjectives for each noun.

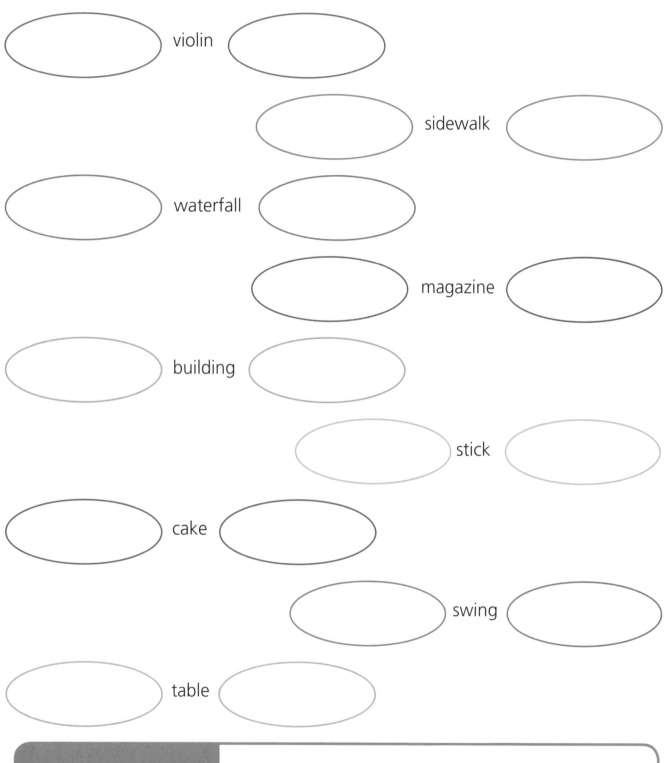

violin

sidewalk

waterfall

magazine

building

stick

cake

swing

table

ON YOUR OWN Write a sentence for each set of words. Use the adjectives you selected or think of new ones!

One Shape, Many Sides

Name the polygon.

1. _____

2. _____

3.  _____

Name the polygon in each everyday object.

4. _____

5.  _____

6.  _____

Now fill in the chart using the information provided. Name the polygon in each everyday object.

Number of Sides	Name	Number of Vertices	Draw Picture
7. 5			
8. 6			
9. 8			

Solar System Crossword

Use the words from the word bank to fill in the blanks.
Do some research to help you.

| eight   revolve   Mercury   rings   sun   ellipse |
| iron   hydrogen   planets   Jupiter |

1. _____ has 63 moons.

2. Four planets are mostly made of _____ and helium.

3. The _____ provides all the heat, light, and energy for the solar system.

4. Each planet orbits the sun in an _____, an oval-shaped path.

5. Four planets are made of _____ and rock.

6. Many _____ have moons that orbit around them.

7. _____ is the closest planet to the sun.

8. Saturn is surrounded by _____.

9. Planets _____ around the sun.

10. Our solar system includes _____ planets.

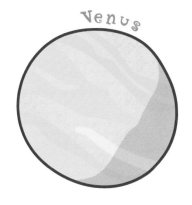

Artful Articles

Color only the stones that contain articles used correctly.

a craft	an umbrella	a unusual event	a garage	an handsome man
a cat	an redwood tree	a knitting needle	a tuba	a contraption
a April shower	a watch	an airplane	a medal	an excuse
a saucer	a antique mirror	a gift	a smile	an curious child
a hair cut	a awful toothache	a pony	a sunset	a parent
a wizard	an bicycle	a stone	a army truck	an honor
a superstar	a tree	an apple	an orignal idea	a history book
a octopus	an awesome ride	an oar	an interesting story	an envelope
an insult	an eggplant	an exciting ending	a car	a friend

Triple Triangles

All triangles have three sides and three vertices, but not all triangles are the same.

Isosceles triangles have two equal sides and two equal angles:

Equilateral triangles have three equal sides and three equal angles:

Right triangles have a right angle:

Answer the questions.

1. Which triangle has three equal sides and three equal angles?_____

2. Which triangle has one 90° angle? _____

3. What kind of a triangle has 2 equal sides and 2 equal angles? _____

4. Can a right triangle have two equal sides and two equal angles?_____

5. Can an equilateral triangle have a right angle? _____

Searching the Solar System

Use at the diagram of the solar system to answer the questions.

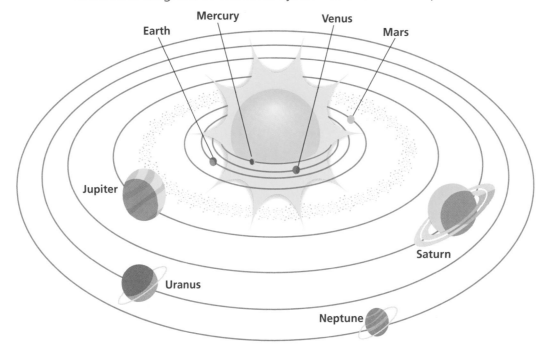

1. In what shape do the planets orbit the sun?

_____

2. How do you think the distance of a planet from the sun affects how long it takes for it to orbit the sun?

_____

_____

3. Which planet do you think is the hottest? Why?

_____

_____

4. Which planet do you think is the coldest? Why?

_____

_____

Nimble Nouns

Each word below can be used as a noun or a verb. Write two sentences for each word. In the first sentence, use the word as a noun. In the second sentence, use the word as a verb.

> **Example:**
>
> The **cook** prepared a delicious turkey.
>
> The turkey will **cook** until it's golden brown and ready to eat.

1. rock _____

_____

2. flock _____

_____

3. fire _____

_____

4. award _____

_____

5. coach _____

_____

6. felt _____

_____

7. stand _____

_____

8. ship _____

_____

Past Tense Practice

Circle the correct past tense form of each verb.

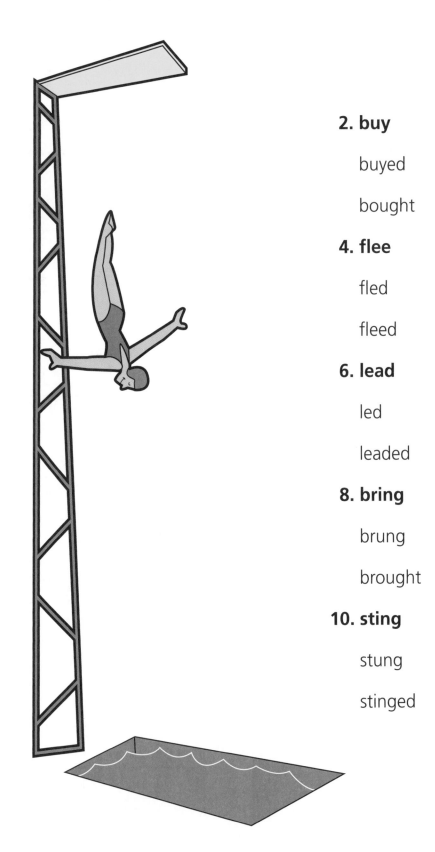

1. dive

dove

doved

2. buy

buyed

bought

3. begin

began

begined

4. flee

fled

fleed

5. grind

grinded

ground

6. lead

led

leaded

7. lose

lost

losed

8. bring

brung

brought

9. shake

shook

shaked

10. sting

stung

stinged

Sure as Shapes

Complete the chart.

	rhombus	rectangle	square	trapezoid
Sets of Parallel Lines				
Number of Right Angles				
Number of Equal Sides				

1. How is a square like a rectangle? _____

2. How is a rhombus like a trapezoid? _____

3. In what way is a rhombus like a square? _____

4. How is a rhombus different from a square? _____

5. Create a drawing using only parallelograms.

What a Day

Sunrise

Midday

Sunset

Use the diagram to answer the questions.

1. How does the position of the sun change during the day? _____

_____

2. At what point is the sun highest above the horizon? _____

_____

3. Describe how the shadows change throughout the day. _____

_____

4. Why does the sun appear to move through the sky during the day? _____

_____

5. Which direction does the sun appear to move through the sky?_____

_____

6. In which direction does the earth rotate? _____

_____

Adverse Adverbs

Write two opposite adverbs for each verb.

1. _____slowly_____ ← walk → _____quickly_____

2. _____ ← run → _____

3. _____ ← swim → _____

4. _____ ← turn → _____

5. _____ ← read → _____

6. _____ ← pedal → _____

7. _____ ← jump → _____

8. _____ ← move → _____

9. _____ ← sing → _____

10. _____ ← blend → _____

11. _____ ← fly → _____

ON YOUR OWN	Use each verb in a sentence. Include at least one of the adverbs in your sentence. Illustrate your work and share it with your friends and family.

Right On with Right Angles

Look at each object. Count the right angles. Write the number on the line.

1.  _____

2.  _____

3.  _____

4.  _____

5. 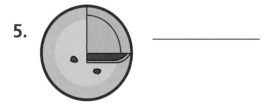 _____

6.  _____

7.  _____

8. 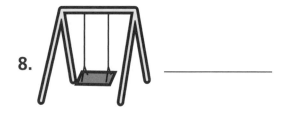 _____

9. 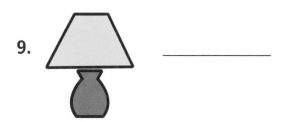 _____

10. 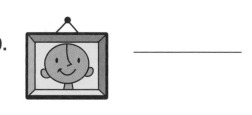 _____

Seasons

The chart below compares average monthly temperatures in Los Angeles, California, and New York, New York. Use the chart to then answer the questions.

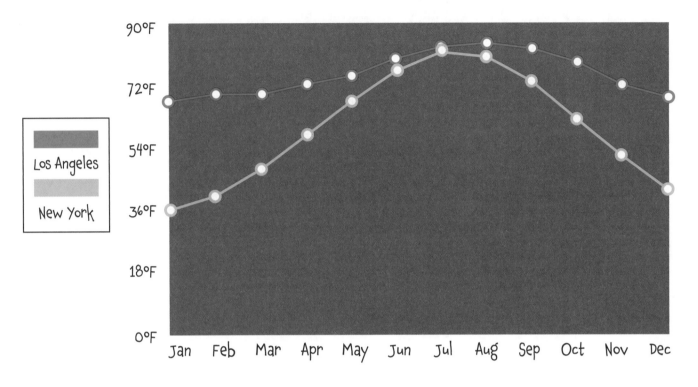

1. What is the average temperature in Los Angeles in April? _____

2. What is the average temperature in New York in October?_____

3. During what season are temperatures in the two cities most similar? _____

   _____

4. During what season are the temperatures most different? _____

   _____

5. In general, which city has the most mild climate? _____

6. Using the Internet, find the average monthly temperatures for your city or town. Add them to the chart. Are the averages in your city closer to the averages in New York or Los Angeles? _____

3-D For Me

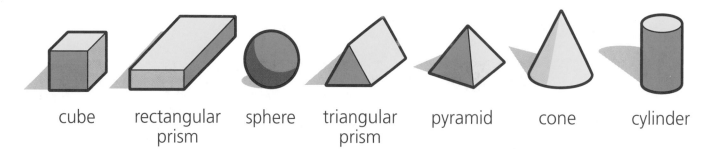

cube | rectangular prism | sphere | triangular prism | pyramid | cone | cylinder

Name the three-dimensional shape.

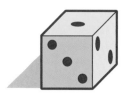

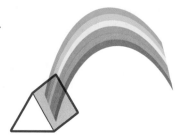

1. _____

2. _____

3. _____

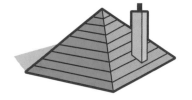

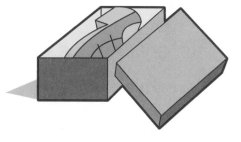

4. _____

5. _____

6. _____

7. List three objects that are shaped like a rectangle. _____

_____

8. List three objects that are shaped like a sphere. _____

_____

9. List three objects that are shaped like a triangle. _____

_____

Favorite Foods

A food chain is an arrangement of plants and animals where each living thing feeds on the one below it. For example, lions are higher in a food chain than zebras, and zebras are higher than grass.

Put each of the following animals in their proper place on the food chain.

Do some research to help you.

1. snake grasshopper hawk toad

_____ ▶ _____ ▶ _____ ▶ _____

2. polar bear shrimp algae seal fish

_____ ▶ _____ ▶ _____ ▶ _____ ▶ _____

3. worm hawk cabbage robin

_____ ▶ _____ ▶ _____ ▶ _____

Now draw your own example of a food chain.

The Hobby Shop

Rewrite the two sentences as one sentence.

> **example:** Jack plays marbles with Victor. Victor is Jack's best friend.
>
> Jack plays marbles with Victor, his best friend.

1. Sara rides her bicycle to Hank's Hobby Shop. Hank's Hobby Shop is Sara's favorite store. _____

_____

2. Raul and Zack trade baseball cards with each other. Raul and Zack are classmates.

_____

_____

3. The radio-controlled car went careening around the backyard. The radio-controlled car is bright blue. _____

_____

4. Ashley enjoys building model airplanes. Ashley enjoys displaying her model airplanes at hobby shows. _____

_____

5. The fire clay was moist and pliable under Janet's hands. The clay was Janet's favorite type to work with. _____

_____

6. Brendan bought three canvases. Brendan wanted to paint. _____

_____

7. Photography is a wonderful hobby. Photography is Margo's favorite thing to do.

_____

_____

Shaping Everything

Name each solid.

1. 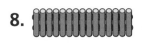 _____

2  _____

3.  _____

4.  _____

5. _____

6.  _____

Identify as many shapes as you see.

7.  _____

8. _____

9.  _____

10. _____

ON YOUR OWN	Design a simple toy using three or more three-dimensional shapes.

169

Craving Carnivores

Carnivores are animals that eat mainly meat. They have sharp, pointy canine teeth used for tearing. These have also heavy skulls and strong jaw muscles used for chewing.

Circle the animals that are carnivores. Choose one to research using the Internet or other resources. Then, on the lines below, write a paragraph about what you learned.

Cool Congruents

Polygons that are the same size and shape are *congruent*.
Circle the shape in each row that is congruent to the red shape.

1.

2.

3.

4.

Draw a congruent shape for each.

5.

6.

7.

8.

Tippy Top Titles

Read each sentence. Underline titles of books, newspapers, magazines, movies, and television shows. Place quotation marks around titles of articles, songs, essays, poems, and stories.

1. I really enjoyed reading the book The Secret Garden by Frances Hodgson Burnett.

2. Every week my mom takes us to the library to hear another chapter of James and the Giant Peach.

3. Emily Dickinson wrote a famous poem called I'm Nobody! Who Are You?

4. Every evening my grandfather reads The Wall Street Journal to get news and information.

5. We are going to the movies to see Monsters vs. Aliens.

6. Aunt Lorna listens to her favorite song, All Shook Up, on my CD player.

7. My essay titled, All Things I See, won first prize in the school essay contest.

8. Will you please record American Idol on TV tonight?

9. Good Housekeeping has been published every month for more than one hundred years.

FAST FACT

Before Johannes Gutenberg invented the printing press in the 1400s, books were copied by hand. The invention of movable type made it much easier and quicker to copy books. Therefore, books became much less expensive and more people could enjoy them!

Mirror Image

A figure that has two halves that mirror each other has bilateral symmetry.

A figure that always looks the same when it's turned has rotational symmetry.

Draw a line to divide each figure and show its bilateral symmetry.

1.   **2.**  **3.**

Tell if the object has rotational symmetry or no rotational symmetry. Write Yes or No.

4. _____ **5.** _____ **6.** _____

Indicate if the object has bilateral symmetry, rotational symmetry, or both.

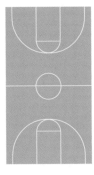 

7. _____ **8.** _____ **9.** _____

You Are What You Eat

Draw a picture of each meal you ate yesterday.

Breakfast

Lunch

Dinner

Are you an omnivore or an herbivore? Explain.

_____

_____

_____

Creepy, Crawly Capitalization

Rewrite each sentence using correct capitalization.

1. the goliath beetle can grow to more than ten Centimeters long.

   _____

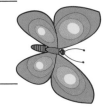

2. ms. rodriguez read a book called *insects: friend or foe* to our class.

   _____

3. Teresa's Dad is an Entomologist, or a scientist who studies insects.

   _____

4. many people in parts of africa eat locusts.

   _____

5. There is a giant ant colony in the vacant lot at 1234 cottonwood street.

   _____

6. Last june, our family visited the insect zoo at the natural history museum in los angeles.

   _____

7. The largest butterfly is Queen Alexandra's birdwing of papua new guinea.

   _____

8. cockroaches smell through their long Antennae.

   _____

Skater Dude

1. Timmy skateboards everyday. He wants to learn how to spin his board 360°. How far around does he have to spin the board to do a "360?" _____

2. What fraction of a circle would a 180° turn be? _____

3. If Timmy made $\frac{1}{4}$ of a turn, what degree of an angle would he have turned the board? _____

4. The final trick Timmy learned before he was able to go all the way around was a "270." What fraction of a turn is required to complete a "270?" _____

5. If Timmy spins his board around two times, how many degrees will he turn?

_____

ON YOUR OWN | Stand facing north. Turn your body 90°. What direction are you facing? Turn your body 180°. Now what direction are you facing?

Deadly Decomposers

Use words or pictures to explain how each of the following is a decomposer.

Fungi

Bacteria

Earthworms

177

Putting It All Together

Tell what each figure will be when put together. Tell how many faces it will have.

Imagine you can fold each shape below to make a solid figure.

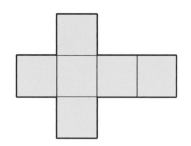

1. _____ _____ faces

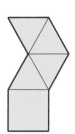

2. _____ _____ faces

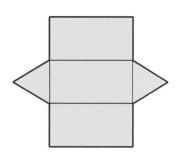

3. _____ _____ faces

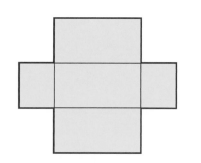

4. _____ _____ faces

ON YOUR OWN

Try copying these shapes onto another sheet of paper. Cut out the shapes and put them together. For a bigger challenge, try enlarging the shape.

That's Impossible!

Circle the likelihood that each event will happen.

1. The sun will come up tomorrow.

likely   certain   unlikely   impossible

2. You could have a whale as a house pet.

likely   certain   unlikely   impossible

3. A child will grow into an adult.

likely   certain   unlikely   impossible

4. Ice cream will taste good.

likely   certain   unlikely   impossible

Read each pair of sentences. Which event is more likely to happen? Circle the sentence.

5. One day your parents will give you an expensive gift for no reason.

On your birthday, your parents will give you a gift.

6. You will get a good grade on a test for which you studied.

You will get a good grade on a test for which you did not study.

Give an example of each.

7. certain _____

8. likely _____

9. unlikely _____

10. impossible _____

Heads I Win!

Use a coin to complete the exercise.

Flip the coin and allow it to land on the floor. Record the side that is facing up. Repeat ten times.

1st time _____   6th time _____

2nd time_____   7th time _____

3rd time _____   8th time _____

4th time _____   9th time _____

5th time _____   10th time _____

Total heads _____   Total tails _____

Answer the questions.

1. How many possible outcomes were there each time you flipped the coin?_____

2. Is it certain that the coin will land on heads?_____

3. Is it impossible to land on heads? _____

4. What kind of graph might you display the data on? _____

ON YOUR OWN	Create a graph of the results.

And the Winner Is . . .

Daniel enjoys recording the daily temperature. He has recorded the high for his town all week. The high temperatures for Daniel's town are:

Monday: 85°, Tuesday: 77°, Wednesday: 76°, Thursday: 80°, Friday: 81°, Saturday: 75°, Sunday: 71°.

Display this information in a line graph.

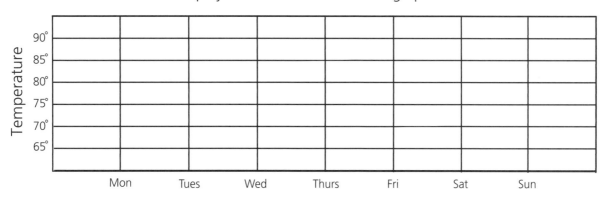

Tannika put three different colored jelly beans in a bag. She made 50 picks out of the bag. She was sure to replace the bean into the bag after she recorded the result. Here were her results:

Red:____**22**____   Blue:____**12**____   Yellow:____**16**____

Make a bar graph to display the results.

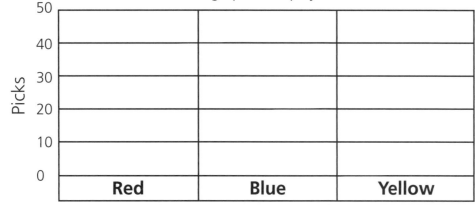

If you were recording the number of students in each grade at your school, would you display them in a bar graph or a line graph? Explain. _____

_____

_____

_____

Measuring Up

Fill in each recipe card to show how much of each ingredient is needed.

Ingredients	1 dozen	5 dozen	12 dozen	15 dozen
shortening	1 cup			
sugar	$1\frac{1}{3}$ cups			
eggs	2			
flour	$3\frac{1}{2}$ cups			
vanilla	2 tsp.			
baking soda	$1\frac{1}{4}$ tsp.			
chocolate chips	$1\frac{3}{4}$ cups			

Pink Lemonade

Ingredients	1 gallon	3 gallons	6 gallons	9 gallons
water	$5\frac{1}{2}$ cups			
sugar	$1\frac{2}{3}$ cups			
lemons	6			
food coloring	$\frac{1}{4}$ tsp.			

Are You a Fan of Chocolate?

Write a question about a flavor of ice cream that has only two possible answers. For example, you might ask, "Is chocolate your favorite ice cream flavor?" The possible answers are "yes" or "no."

Ask ten people the question and record their answers using tally marks.

Yes _____

No _____

What kind of graph would best display the results of the data? _____

Make a graph to display the results. Remember to have a title and labels.

It is All About the Data

The number that appears most often in a set of data is called the mode. The median is the middle number in a set of data when it is put in numerical order. If there are two middles, the median is the average of the two numbers. An outlier is an item that doesn't seem to fit in the range of the other data.

Put the scores in order from least to greatest.

70%	
91%	
99%	
92%	
92%	
95%	
92%	

1. What is the mode in this data set?_____

2. What is the median? _____

3. Is there an outlier in this set of data? What is it?_____

4. What might explain the lowest test score? _____

_____

Back to School

Data can be compared in graphs. The graphs tell the boys' favorite 4th grade subject and the girls' favorite subject. Use the graphs to answer the questions.

Boys

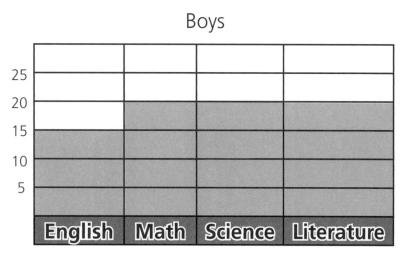

Girls

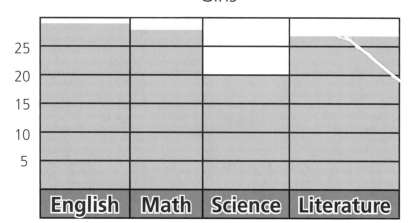

1. Do more boys or girls like English?_____

2. Do more girls like math or science? _____

3. What subject is the boys' least favorite?_____

4. About the same number of boys and girls like which subject? _____

5. What is your favorite subject? _____

Answer Key

Page 4
1. fight
2. delight
3. flight
4. slight
5. fright
6. might
7. sight
8. bright
9. tight
10. light

Page 5
2. seventy-five
3. six thousand three hundred seventy-five
4. one thousand two hundred eighty-six
5. six thousand six hundred four
6. four thousand seventy
8. 9,989, nine thousand nine hundred eighty-nine
9. 5,041, five thousand forty-one
11. 3,199, three thousand one hundred ninety-nine
12. 6,374, six thousand three hundred seventy-four

Page 6
1. using a solar cell; collecting heat using mirrors
2. watches, calculators, spacecraft, satellites
3. in a place that cannot be reached by power lines
4. Answers will vary.

Page 7
1. plural
2. furniture
3. benefit
4. calculate
5. dispute
6. experience
7. molecule
8. consonant
9. necessary
10. temperature
11. substance
12. particular

Page 8
1. <
2. >
3. <
4. =
5. <
6. <
7. >
8. =
9. <
10. >
11. 66
12. 4,749
13. 752
14. 8,621
15. 3,101
16. 7,001
17. 1,198
18. 1,000
19. 9,999
20. 49

Page 9
1. desert
2. gulf
3. forest
4. ocean
5. hill
6. peninsula
7. island
8. valley
9. lake

Page 10
Answers will vary, but should use both homophones correctly.

Page 11
1. 6,001   6,075   6,571   6,751
2. 2,005   2,045   2,405   2,450
3. 3,900   3,390   3,339   3,039
4. 7,707   7,177   7,107   7,077
5. 37,501
6. 987; 1,001; 1,299; 10,001; 10,299.
7. 3,997;   3,967;   3,566;   3,506

Page 12
1. potential
2. kinetic
3. potential
4. kinetic
5. potential
6. kinetic
7. potential
8. kinetic

Page 13

melt — dissolve
appetizing — delicious
stale — spoiled
fresh — new
plain — ordinary
raw — uncooked
charred — burned
creamy — smooth
mix — blend
slice — cut
eat — nibble
hungry — satisfied
full — famished

Page 14
1. ones
2. tens
3. thousands
4. hundreds
5. ten thousands
6.-9. Answers will vary.

Page 15
1. Population of various countries
2. 300,000,000
3. Greenland
4. Nigeria
5. China and India
6. Answers will vary but might include lack of food and services, overcrowding.

Page 16

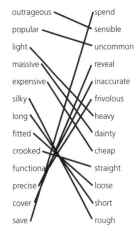

outrageous — sensible
popular — uncommon
light — heavy
massive — dainty
expensive — cheap
silky — rough
long — short
fitted — loose
crooked — straight
functional — frivolous
precise — inaccurate
cover — reveal
save — spend

Page 17
1. 1,680; 1,700; 2,000
2. 9,810; 9,800; 10,000
3. 13,390; 13,400; 13,000
4. 99,132; 99,130; 99,100; 99,000

Page 18
1. windmills grind grain; water creates electricity for homes and buildings; solar power can be used to run big and small things
2. These resources cannot be used up. They are readily available and easy to find.
3. Answers will vary.

Page 19
1. feeling uncomfortable
2. tell me what your are thinking
3. don't put all your resources in one place
4. back to the beginning
5. feeling nervous
6. making things worse
7. feeling sick
1.-7. Sentences will vary.

Page 20
1. 384,400; 384,400; 384,000; 380,000; 400,000
2. 376,540; 376,500; 377,000; 380,000; 400,000
3. 11,404,800; 11,404,800; 11,405,000; 11,400,000; 11,400,000

Page 21
Drawings and paragraphs will vary.

Page 22
1. heir
2. banned
3. shoot
4. dough
5. aunt
6. idol
7. poll
8. wrung
9. eight
10. board
11. cord
12. deer
13. dye
14. might
15. metal
16. knot
17. daze
18. creak

Page 23
1. estimate; 160,000
2. estimate; 200; yes
3. estimate; 26
4. exact; $2,654,532
5. exact; 439
6. estimate; $200,000

Page 24
1. The object didn't move.
2. The water got wavy.
3. The object moved up and down over the waves.
4. The waves caused the object to move.
5. The waves transfer energy to the objects on or in them.

Page 25
Sentences will vary.

Page 26
1. 500 + 30 + 6
2. 700 + 90 + 3
3. 400 + 40 + 1 = $441
4. 200 + 9 = $209
5. 1,000 + 500 + 80 + 0
6. Answers will vary, for example: 500 + 50 + 5 = 555

Page 27
Answers will vary.

Page 28
misadventure
miscalculate
mislead
misplace
misfortune
biathlon
biceps
bicycle
bicentennial
biped
biplane
binocular
unafraid
unclogged
uneaten
unimportant
unmistakably

Page 29
1. negative
2. positive
3. one
4. four
5. seven
6. -1°
7. 8°
8. 2°
9. Answers will vary.

Page 30
Paragraphs will vary.

Page 31
1. a writer or author
2. a gardener
3. an actor
4. a teacher or professor
5. a doctor
6. a surfer
7. Answers will vary.

Page 32
1. 7,770
2. 43,612
3. 111,161
4. 44,356
5. 86,979
6. 100,000
7. 18,750
8. 56,180
9. 98,880
10. $80,329

Page 35
Paragraphs will vary but should include information on how the tribe lived, how it ruled, its government, and any important historical information.

Page 36
Synonyms and antonyms will vary.

Page 37
1. 3,611
2. 3,650
3. 20,664
4. 76,772
5. 2,109
6. 57,996
7. 23,439
8. 26,661
9. 42,078
10. 3,042
11. 11,276
12. $71,843
13. 3,330

Page 38

Page 39
1. growl or thundered
2. huge, extremely large
3. moved
4. moving swiftly

Page 40
First Race

12	12	40
18	24	28
15	24	56
81	35	27
81	486	340
576	68	616
220	441	245

Second Race

63	0	36
42	5	49
14	64	45
32	54	42
584	160	279
261	380	492
296	38	196

Page 41
1. They traveled across the ice sheets over what is now the Bering Strait.
2. Hunters and farmers, and sophisticated cities and governments
3. Europeans tried to get the Indians to change their way of life. Europeans introduced new diseases. Europeans fought the Indians for land.

Page 42
Words should be in this order: lime, limerick, limit, limousine, limp, line. Definitions will vary.

Page 43

Page 44
Observations and results will vary.

Page 45
Sentences will vary but should use each word with two different meanings.

Page 46
1. 625
2. 3,750
3. 1,585
4. 243
5. 496
6. 9,408
7. 2,175
8. 12,500

Page 47
Brochures will vary.

Page 48
1. c
2. a
3. c
4. b

Page 49
1. 73
2. 214
3. 24
4. 1,239
5. 1,239
6. 613
7. 277
8. Answers will vary.

Page 50
Answers will vary.

Page 51
1. Wear protective gear, find skates that fit, start slowly.
2. Wear a hat, and wear sunscreen.

Page 52
1. Answers will vary.
2. Answers will vary.
3. Any number divided by one equals itself.
4. Zero; any number multiplied by zero is zero.
5. no
6. Zero divided by zero is zero.

Page 53
Answers will vary.

Page 54
Predictions will vary but should include a reason why.

Page 55
1. 0.55
2. 1.20
3. 3.60
4. 1.92
5. 0.23
6. 3.29
7. 3.09
8. 0.09
9. 3.99
10. 4.65

Page 56
Answers will vary but may include:
Definition: the smallest component of an element
How scientist view atoms: through a microscope
Where are atoms found? in every piece of matter

Page 57
1. Answers will vary.
2. Pocahontas was an important woman in the relationship between Native Americans and Europeans.
3. She saved the life of John Smith and worked to improve the relationship between Europeans and Native Americans.
4. Sacagawea was an important woman in the Lewis and Clark expedition.
5. She had connections in both European and Native American worlds. She helped Lewis and Clark get horses and safe passage.

Page 58
2.
3.
4.

Page 59
Answers will vary.

Page 60
1. Suddenly, his shoe lace got caught in the chain.
2. She didn't have any milk.
3. They didn't have any matches to light the fire.
4. They needed to get the Pedro's house in one hour for the lemonade stand.
5. As she put the board down, she noticed the neighbor's dog running off down the street without his owner.
1.-5. Solutions will vary.

Page 61
1. $\frac{1}{2}$ cup
2. 1 hour
3. $\frac{5}{8}$
4. $\frac{5}{6}$
5. $\frac{3}{5}$
6. $\frac{7}{12}$
7. $\frac{4}{9}$
8. $\frac{3}{5}$

Page 62
Paragraphs will vary.

Page 63
Games will vary.

Page 64
1. $\frac{1}{2}$
2. $\frac{1}{6}$
3. $\frac{2}{3}$
4. $\frac{1}{4}$
5. $\frac{5}{6}$
6. $\frac{1}{3}$
7. $\frac{1}{3}$
8. $\frac{1}{5}$

Page 65
Answers will vary.

Page 66
1. Sally Ride
2. Ride's Early Life
3. What she had to do to become an astronaut or what happened while she was an astronaut.
4. Sally Ride was the first American female to travel in space.

Page 67
1. $\frac{2}{2} = 1$
2. $\frac{2}{3}$
3. $\frac{2}{4} = \frac{1}{2}$
4. $\frac{4}{8} = \frac{1}{2}$
5. $\frac{4}{6} = \frac{2}{3}$
6. $\frac{2}{8} = \frac{1}{4}$
7. $\frac{3}{12} = \frac{1}{4}$
8. $\frac{5}{10} = \frac{1}{2}$
9. $\frac{5}{5} = 1$
10. $\frac{6}{12} = \frac{1}{2}$

Page 68
Answers will vary.

Page 69
1. plaque
2. They form plaque.
3. It eats away at the enamel.
4. It could die.

Page 70
2. $\frac{1}{3}$; parts of a whole
3. $\frac{3}{7}$; parts of a set
4. $\frac{6}{10}$; parts of a set
5. $\frac{4}{8}$; parts of a whole
6. $\frac{2}{6}$; parts of a set

Page 71
1. the names and numbers of all the elements
2. alkaline earth
3. metaloid
4. nonmetal
5. Answers will vary.

Page 72
1. Matisse moved to Paris as a young man.
2. Matisse experimented with the effects of light.
3. Matisse painted abstracts on the coast of the Mediterranean Sea.
4. Matisse showed his work at the Autumn Salon.
5. Matisse was influenced by Islamic architecture and art.
6. Matisse used paper cutouts in his art.

Page 73
1. 3; three-tenths; $\frac{3}{10}$
2. $\frac{9}{10}$
3. $\frac{42}{100}$
4. .63
5. .10; one-tenth
6. ninety-one hundreths; $\frac{91}{100}$
7. .1; $\frac{10}{100}$
8. six hundreths; $\frac{6}{100}$
9. .09; nine hundreths
10. one; $\frac{1}{1}$
12. 2.25
13. 1.5
14. 1.75
15. 2

Page 74
Ads will vary.

Page 75
Facts and questions will vary.

Page 76
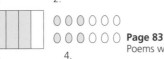

Page 77
Answers will vary but should include some of the following information:
1. The shadow was little.
2. The shadow was longer.
3. They were different sizes.
4. An object is between the sun and the ground, blocking the sunlight.
5. The sun was in a different position in the sky.

Page 78
Answers will vary.

Page 79
Answers will vary.

Page 80
1. $0.40
2. $0.40
3. $0.30
4. $2.60
5. $10.00
6. $3.90
7. $8.00
8. $17.00
9. $22.00
10. $40.00
11. $100.00
12. $45.00
13. $4.10; $4.00
14. $5.80; $6.00
15. $5.50; $5.00
16. $9.00; $9.00
17. $48.80; $49.00
18. $200.00; $200.00

Page 81
Answers will vary but should all express an opinion.

Page 82
1. $2.10
2. $4.38
3. $6.59
4. $4.16
5. $3.70
6. $2.68

Page 83
Poems will vary.

Page 84
Instructions will vary.

Page 85
1. $52.64
2. $9.00
3. $6.56
4. $12.00
5. $14.11
6. $344.00

Page 86
Pictures will vary.

Page 87
Holidays: Christmas Around the World, Winter Celebrations, Diwali: Festival of Lights
Making friends: How to Make People Laugh; Fun Activities to Do with Friends; My Best Friend Jerry
Summer vacation: The Happy Days of Summer; Summer in the Sun; What I Did on Vacation
Families: The Story of Our Family; A Family in Need; Family Fun

Page 88
1. $3.00 x 4 = $12.00
2. $6.20 x 5 = $31.00
3. $11.15 x 7 = $78.05
4. $13.87 x 9 = $124.83
5. $20.01 x 8 = $160.08
6. $91.76 x 3 = $275.28
7. $34.08 x 2 = $68.16
8. $ 75.33 x 6 = $451.98
9. $17.00
10. $7.50
11. $76.05
12. $40.00

Page 89
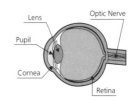

Page 90
Answers will vary.

Page 91
1. $15.00 ÷ 3 = $5.00
2. $40.00 ÷ 8 = $5.00
3. $48.00 ÷ 6 = $8.00
4. $357.28 ÷ 4 = $89.32
5. $462.00 ÷ 7 = $66
6. $56.97 ÷ 9 = $6.33
7. $34.02 ÷ 3 = $11.34
8. $67.00 ÷ 5 = $13.40
9. $5.00
10. $9.00
11. $10.00
12. $36.29; $2.42

Page 92
Answers will vary.

Page 93
1. an Italian restaurant
2. an outdoor basketball court
3. on a dock at the lake
4. a library

Page 94
1. 1 + 1 + 1 = 3 backpacks
2. 2 x 5 = 10 shots
3. 2 x 3 = 6 bottles
4. 3 + 5 = 8 hikers
5. 5 children + 3 adults = 8 people
6. 5 children x 2 cookies = 10 cookies

Page 95
1. The electricity in a series circuit flows through all the bulbs.
2. If the flow of electricity is interrupted, none of the bulbs will work because the circuit has been broken.
3. If more bulbs are added the light will be dimmer on each bulb because they have to share the same amount of electricity between them.

Page 96
1. The main character is Tamika.
2. Tamika dances. She practices. She learns. She dreams of being on Broadway.
3. Tamika says she wants to be on stage.
4. Answers will vary.

Page 97
1. Yes; 8.00 + 8.00 = 16.00 < 20.00
2. 53 X 2 = 106 pounds
3. 400 ÷ 5 = 80 fans
4. 35 + 6 = 41÷ 25 = 1.64; 2 buses
5. 6 x 2 = 12
12 x $5.00 = $60.00

Page 98
Paragraphs will vary but should include most of the given facts.

Page 99
Fables should have animals as characters and should include a lesson or moral.

Page 100
4 x 3 = 12
5 + 2 = 7
17 – 6 = 11
10 ÷ 2 = 5
16 – 8 = 8
3 + 4 = 7
6 x 8 = 48
9 x 7 = 63
121 ÷ 11 = 11
75 + 6 = 81
125 – 25 = 100
11 x 12 = 132
144 ÷ 12 = 12
37 + 13 = 50
432 ÷ 9 = 48

Page 101
Answers will vary.

Page 102
Legends will vary but should be based on fact.

Page 103
1. 12 inches = 1 foot
2. 36 inches = 3 feet
3. 72 inches = 6 feet
4. 108 inches = 9 feet
5. 144 inches = 12 feet
6. 3 feet = 1 yard
7. 6 feet = 2 yards
8. 66 feet = 22 yards
9. 108 feet = 36 yards
10. 366 feet = 122 yards
11. 5,280 feet = 1 mile
12. 15,840 feet = 3 miles
13. 52,800 feet = 10 miles
14. 126,720 feet = 24 miles
15. 264,000 feet = 50 miles

Page 104
Down
1. speaking
2. escaped
4. freed
7. underground
Across
1. slave
3. captured
5. abolition
6. Lincoln

Page 105
Descriptions will vary but should include a lot of detail.

Page 106
If 3 x 4 = 12, then 4 x 3 = 12
If 2 x 8 = 16, then 8 x 2 = 16
If 4 x 2 = 8 then 2 x 4 = 8
If 1 x 9 = 9, then 9 x 1 = 9
If 3 x 2 = 6, then 2 x 3= 6
If 5 x 9 = 45, then 9 x 5 = 45
If 3 x 7 = 21, then 7 x 3 = 21
If 2 x 6 = 12, then 6 x 2 = 12
If 4 x 9 = 36, then 9 x 4 = 36
If 5 x 3 = 15, then 3 x 5 =15

Page 107
Kaley: Cobb salad; Judah: chicken; Brooke: hamburger; Asher: steak; Ali: pizza; Delia: lasagna.

Page 108
1. Saturday, June 30
2. 8 AM to 3 PM
3. four families
4. Cypress Grove Road
5. yes
6. no

Page 109
1. If 2 x 4 x 3 = 24, then
   3 x 4 x 2 = 24
2. If 6 x 1 x 2 = 12, then
   2 x 1 x 6 = 12
3. If 9 x 2 x 3 = 54, then
   3 x 2 x 9 = 54
4. If 2 x 2 x 6 = 24, then
   2 x 6 x 2 = 24
5. If 5 x 3 x 7 = 105, then
   7 x 3 x 5 = 105
6. If 3 x 9 x 4 = 108, then
   9 x 3 x 4 = 108
7. If 2 x 3 x 8 = 48, then
   3 x 2 x 8 = 48
8. If 9 x 1 x 7 = 63, then
   7 x 1 x 9 = 63
9. If 4 x 5 x 3 = 60, then
   3 x 5 x 4 = 60
10. If 8 x 7 x 4 = 224, then
   4 x 7 x 8 = 224
Pictures will vary.

Page 110
Posters will vary.

Page 111
Similes and metaphors will vary.

Page 112
The product of 892 x 6 plus the product of 892 x 30 is the same and the product of 892 x 36.
1. 482 x 26 = 12,532

   482 x 20 = 9,640
   482 x 6 = 2,892
   9,640 + 2,892 = 12,532
2. 5,150 x 29 = 149,350

   5,150 x 20 = 103,000
   5,150 x 9 = 46350
   103,000 + 46,350 = 149,350
3. 5,844 x 16 = 93,504

   5,844 x 10 = 58,440
   5,844 x 6 = 35,064
   58,440 + 35,064 = 93,504

Page 113
1. a community of living things
2. a characteristic that allows an animal to survive in its environment
3. a parrotfish uses its beak to scrape food from rocks; an eels thin body makes it easy to swim through narrow cracks in the reef
4. a relationship where one animal helps another
5. wrasses feed on the parasites from larger fish

Page 114
Scripts will vary.

Page 115
1. .75 x 12 = $9.00
2. 1.49 x 18 = $26.82
3. 3.01 x 9 = $27.09
4. 6.74 x 2 = $13.48
5. 2.39 x 6 = $14.34
6. .82 x 3 = $2.46

Page 116
1961 born in Honolulu, Hawaii to parents Ann Dunham and Barack Obama, Sr.
1967 Moved to Indonesia with his mother and stepfather.
1971 Returned to Hawaii to attend Punahou School in Honolulu.
1983 Graduated from Columbia University
1991 Graduated from Harvard Law School and was selected to be president of the Harvard Law Review
1992 Married Michelle Robinson
1996 Elected to the Illinois Senate where he helped to change rules about police procedures and ethics violations.
2004 Elected to the United State Senate in an overwhelming win over

Alan Keyes
2008 Elected president of the United States

Page 117
Paragraphs will vary.

Page 118
1. 4 x 2 = 8; or 2 + 2 + 2 + 2 = 8
2. 8 x 8 = 64; or 8 + 8 + 8 + 8 + 8 + 8 + 8 + 8 = 64
3. 3 x 5 = 15; or 5 + 5 + 5 = 15
4. 3 x 4 = 12; 4 + 4 + 4 = 12
5. 9 x 2 = 18; or 2 + 2 + 2 + 2 + 2 + 2 + 2 + 2 + 2 = 18

Page 119
1. thick stems; waxy skin; long, thick roots
2. spines
3.- 4. Answers will vary.

Page 120
Answers will vary.

Page 121
1. scale
2. measuring cup
3. ruler
4. length
5. weight/mass
6. volume
7.- 9. Answers will vary.

Page 122
1. A producer is a person or company that makes something for sale. Possible example: The Ford Motor Company is a producer of cars.
2. A consumer is a person who buys a product. Possible example: A person who buys a car from the Ford Motor company is a consumer.

Page 123
Drafts will vary but should include similar ideas grouped into paragraphs.

Page 124
1. scale
2. meter stick
3. measuring cup
4. ruler
5. tape measure
6. scale
7. measuring cup
8. scale
9. measuring cup
10. odometer

Page 125
Answers will vary.

Page 126
Paragraphs will vary but should include revisions that improve upon writing on page 123.

Page 127
1. 75 cubic units
2. 8 cubic units
3. 36 cubic units
4. 50 cubic inches
5. 80 cubic centimeters
6. 96 cubic feet

Page 128
Answers will vary.

Page 129
Essays will vary but should show that mistakes in spelling, grammar, and punctuation on page 126 have been corrected.

Page 130
1. 355 mL volume
2. 560 g mass
3. 12 m length
4. 91 m length
5. 1,200 kg mass
6. 2 m length
7. 10 L volume
8. 57 L volume
9. 1 m length
10. 1 kg mass

Page 131

Page 132
Drawings will vary.

Page 133
1. inches
2. ounces
3. ounces
4. inches
5. gallons
6. pound
7. inches
8. pounds
9. pounds
10. yards
11.- 15. Answers will vary but should include correct measurements.

Page 134
Money earned: $55
Money spent: $30
Money saved: $25
1. 12 months
2. $5\frac{1}{2}$ months

Page 135
Answers will vary but should include sensory details.

Page 136
1. 9 square units
2. 12 square units
3. 15 square units
4. 60 square centimeters
5. 35 square units
6. 36 square feet

Page 137
Stories will vary.

Page 138
Letters will vary.

Page 139
1. square; 12 cm
2. hexagon; 24 cm
3. rhombus; 12 cm
4. octagon; 16 cm
5. pentagon; 10 cm
6. triangle; 21 cm

Page 140
1. State drained water from the land to make farms. Later, water was taken to supply drinking water to growing cities. Chemicals from farms leaked into the water, hurting plants and animals.
2. The government designated the area as a national park.
3. Essays will vary.

Page 141
Letters will vary but should include a date, salutation, body, closing, and signature.

Page 142
1. 2 ft = 24 in
2. 13 lb = 208 oz
3. 60 in = 5 ft
4. 3 c = 24 oz
5. 20 oz = 1 lb 4oz
6. 400 cm = 4 m
7. 5 kg =   5,000 g
8. 10 L = 10,000 mL
9. 1,000 g = 1 kg
10. 25 m = 250 cm

Page 143
Mercury 36 million miles
Venus 67.2 million miles
Earth 93 million miles
Mars 141,620,000 miles
Jupiter 484 million miles
Saturn 890,750,000 miles
Uranus 1,784,860,000 miles
Neptune 2,793,100,000 miles
Charactersistics will vary but can include gaseous composition, length of days, and length of year.

Page 144
1. declarative
2. declarative
3. interrogative
4. imperative
5. exclamatory
6. declarative
7. declarative
8. declarative
9. imperative
10. interrogative
11. declarative
12. exclamatory

Page 145
1. A= 12; P=14
2. A= 12; P=16
3. A=12; P=26
4. A=20; P=24
5. A=20; P=18
6. A=20; P=42

Page 146
Poems will vary.

Page 147
1. The train roars into the station.
2. The conductor shouts "All aboard!"
3. Passengers scramble to get on the train.
4. Luggage is hauled into the storage compartment.
5. Kenisha and Trent are very excited to pull out of the station.
6. The giant engine rumbles as the wheels begin to turn.
7. The sleek train speeds along the track.
8. Kenisha looks out the window.
9. Trent takes a picture.
10. They feel happy to be on their first train ride.

Page 148
1. P= 18 inches; A= 20 square inches
2. P=18 centimeters; A= 14 square centimeters
3. P= 38 yards; A= 18 square yards
4. P =24 feet; A= 32 square feet
5. P=24 inches; A=36 square inches
6. P=24 miles; A=20 square miles

Page 149
1. b
2. a
3. a
4. c

Page 150
1. d
2. b
3. c
4. a
5. c

Page 151

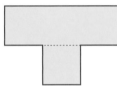

1. 3 square units; 1square unit
2. 4 square units
3. Answers will vary.

Page 152

Page 153
Answers will vary.

Page 154
1. octagon
2. hexagon
3. pentagon
4. hexagon
5. pentagon
6. octagon

Number of Sides	Name	Number of Vertices	Draw Picture
7. 5	Pentagon	5	
8. 6	Hexagon	6	
9. 8	Octagon	8	

Page 155
1. Jupiter
2. hydrogen
3. sun
4. ellipses
5. iron
6. planets
7. Mercury
8. rings
9. revolve
10. eight

Page 156

Page 157
1. equilateral triangle
2. right triangle
3. isosceles traiangle
4. yes
5. no

Page 158
1. oval or ellipses
2. The further away the planet is, the longer it takes to orbit because the ellipses is larger.
3. Mercury because it is closest to the sun.
4. Neptune because it is furthest from the sun.

Page 159
Sentences will vary but should use each word as a noun and then a verb.

Page 160
1. dove
2. bought
3. began
4. fled
5. ground
6. led
7. lost
8. brought
9. shook
10. stung

Page 161

	rhombus	rectangle	square	trapezoid
Sets of Parallel Lines	2	2	2	1
Number of Right Angles	0	4	4	0
Number of Equal Sides	2	2	4	0

1. two sets of parallel sides
2. no right angles
3. four equal sides
4. rhombus has no right angles
5. Drawings will vary.

Page 162
1. It moves from east to west.
2. midday
3. When the sun is lower on the horizon, the shadows are longer. When the sun is high overhead, the shadows are shorter.
4. Because the earth is rotating on its axis.
5. east to west
6. west to east

Page 163
Answers will vary but should include pairs of antonym adverbs.

Page 164
1. 4
2. 0
3. 2
4. 16
5. 1
6. 1
7. 4
8. 8
9. 0
10. 4

Page 165
1. about 73 degrees
2. about 64 degrees
3. summer
4. winter
5. Los Angeles
6. Answers will vary.

Page 166
1. cone
2. sphere
3. triangular prism
4. cube
5. pyramid
6. rectangular prism
7. Answers will vary.
8. Answers will vary.
9. Answers will vary.

Page 167
1. grasshopper, toad, snake, hawk
2. algae, shrimp, fish, seal, polar bear
3. cabbage, worm, robin, hawk

Page 168
Sentences can be combined multiple ways. Possibilities include:
1. Sara rides her bicycle to her favorite store, Hank's Hobby Shop.
2. Classmates Raul and Zack trade baseball cards with each other.
3. The bright blue radio-controlled car went careening around the backyard.
4. Ashley enjoys building model airplanes and displaying them at hobby shows.
5. The fire clay, Janet's favorite type, felt moist and pliable under her hands.
6. Brendan wanted to paint, so he bought three canvases.
7. Photography, a wonderful hobby, is Margo's favorite thing to do.

Page 169
1. sphere
2. pyramid
3. rectangular prism
4. cube
5. cylinder
6. triangular prism
7. rectangular prism, cylinder
8. cylinders
9. sphere, cube
10. triangular prism, rectangular prisim

Page 170

Paragraphs will vary but can include the following; Food: prey on other animals; meat
Physical Characteristics: sharp teeth, strong jaw,
Examples: bears, hyenas, wolves, lions, and many others

Page 171

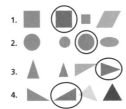

1.
2.
3.
4.
5.- 8. Shapes should be identical

Page 172
1. I really enjoyed reading the book The Secret Garden by Frances Hodgson Burnett.
2. Every week my mom takes us to the library to hear another chapter of James and the Giant Peach.
3. Emily Dickinson wrote a famous poem called "I'm Nobody! Who Are You?"
4. Every evening my grandfather reads the Wall Street Journal to get news and information.
5. We are going to the movies to see Monsters vs. Aliens.
6. Aunt Lorna listens to her favorite song, "All Shook Up," on my CD player.
7. My essay titled, "All Things I See," won first prize in the school essay contest.
8. Will you please record American Idol on TV tonight?
9. Good Housekeeping has been published every month for more than one hundred years.

Page 173

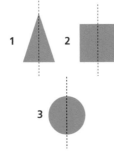

1
2
3
4. yes
5. no
6. no
7. bilateral symmetry
8. both
9. bilateral symmetry

Page 174
Answers will vary.

Page 175
1. The Goliath beetle can grow to more than ten centimeters long.
2. Ms. Rodriguez read a book called Insects: Friend or Foe to our class.
3. Teresa's dad is an entomologist, or a scientist who studies insects.
4. Many people in parts of Africa eat locusts.
5. There is a giant ant colony in the vacant lot at 1234 Cottonwood Street.
6. Last June, our family visited the Insect Zoo at the Natural History Museum in Los Angeles.
7. The largest butterfly is Queen Alexandra's birdwing of Papua New Guinea.
8. Cockroaches smell through their long antennae.

Page 176
1. a full circle
2. $\frac{1}{2}$
3. 90°
4. $\frac{3}{4}$
5. 720°

Page 177
Fungi: release enzymes that decompose plants and animals that have died and fallen to the ground
Bacteria: microscopic organisms that breakdown food, dead plants, and dead animals
Earthworms: eat dead plants and animals, excrete waste which is full of nutrients

Page 178
1. cube; 6
2. pyramid; 5
3. triangular prism; 5
4. rectangular prism; 6

Page 179
1. certain
2. impossible
3. certain
4. likely
5. On your birthday, your parents will give you a gift.
6. You will get a good grade on a test for which you studied.
7. Answers will vary.
8. Answers will vary.
9. Answers will vary.
10. Answers will vary.

Page 180
1. 2
2. no
3. no
4. bar or pie graph

Page 181

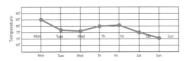

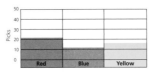

Page 182

Chocolate Cupcakes				
Ingredients	1 dozen	5 dozen	12 dozen	15 dozen
shortening	1 cup	5 cups	12 cups	15 cups
sugar	1$\frac{1}{3}$ cup	6$\frac{2}{3}$ cups	16 cups	20 cups
eggs	2	10	24	30
flour	3$\frac{1}{2}$ cups	17$\frac{1}{2}$ cups	42 cups	52$\frac{1}{2}$ cups
vanilla	2 tsp.	10 tsp.	24 tsp.	30 tsp.
baking soda	1$\frac{1}{4}$ tsp.	6$\frac{1}{4}$ tsp.	15 tsp.	18$\frac{3}{4}$ tsp.
chocolate chips	1$\frac{3}{4}$ cups	8$\frac{3}{4}$ cups	21 cups	26$\frac{1}{4}$ cups

Pink Lemonade				
Ingredients	1 gallon	3 gallons	6 gallons	9 gallons
water	5$\frac{1}{2}$ cups	16$\frac{1}{2}$ cups	33 cups	49$\frac{1}{2}$ cups
sugar	1$\frac{2}{3}$ cups	5 cups	10 cups	15 cups
lemons	6	18	36	54
food coloring	$\frac{1}{4}$ tsp.	$\frac{3}{4}$ tsp.	1$\frac{1}{2}$ tsp.	2$\frac{1}{4}$ tsp.

Page 183
Answers will vary but should express information in a clearly labeled graph.

Page 184
70%
91%
92%
92%
92%
95%
99%
1. 92%
2. 92%
3. yes, 70%
4. Answers will vary.

Page 185
1. girls
2. math
3. math
4. science
5. Answers will vary.